Tales from the Cockpit

John McCollister

Sports Publishing L.L.C.
www.SportsPublishingLLC.com

© 2003 John McCollister
All Rights Reserved.

Direction of production: Susan M. Moyer
Project manager: Greg Hickman
Developmental editor: Cynthia L. McNew
Copy editor: Cynthia L. McNew
Dust jacket design: Joseph Brumleve

ISBN: 1-58261-659-0

Printed in the United States.

SPORTS PUBLISHING L.L.C.
www.SportsPublishingLLC.com

This book is dedicated to author, lecturer, and humorist Robert J. Serling, with appreciation for his half-century of enthusiastic support of aviation.

Acknowledgments

The poet/philosopher John Donne once wrote, "No man is an island." The same holds true in the world of aviation. Any pilot who sits in the left seat of any aircraft—a Boeing 747, an F-16, or a Cessna 172—dare never think that he or she is the Lone Ranger. Worthy pilots remain alert for other aircraft and heed instructions from air traffic controllers. And, like it or not, they comply with rules and regulations established by the FAA and other governmental bodies. Gathering input from all of these sources gives each pilot the best chance for a successful flight.

The same logic applies to writing a book. No author—especially this one—can hope to produce the best possible product by flying solo. He's best advised to seek input from others who have "been there and done that." Among those who have contributed to these tales are award-winning author Robert J. Serling (*The President's Plane is Missing*), author Robert Gandt (*Acts of Vengeance*), American Airlines Captain John T. McCollister (no relation to the author, a fact eagerly endorsed by both parties), retired TWA Captain Jack Clary, Dr. Robert T. Chilcoat, Jim Foreman, former astronaut and airline executive Frank Borman, plus the fraternity of the Spruce Creek Fly-In Four O'Clock Happy Hour.

Finally, the author gives a standing ovation to Sports Publishing L.L.C. for its willingness to include *Tales From the Cockpit* among its treasured collection. There's good reason for their decision, however, as none other than Wilbur Wright proclaimed nearly a century ago:

"The exhilaration of flying is too keen, the pleasure too great, for it to be neglected as a sport."

—John McCollister

Contents

Introduction vi

Part 1:
The Pioneers 1

Part 2:
When Airplanes Went to War 27

Part 3:
The Presidents 53

Part 4:
Stars Among the Stars 62

Part 5:
Our Healthy Respect for Flying 90

Part 6:
Communications 100

Part 7:
Aviation Characters 130

Part 8:
Parables 145

Part 9:
The Feds 152

Part 10:
Our Beautiful (and sometimes not so beautiful) Birds ... 161

Part 11:
Vision 169

Introduction

Had he known my grandfather, Aesop would have been a better storyteller.

My grandfather, William Lyman Hall, was part of a lost generation—those who honed the ability to spin a yarn. Through vivid descriptions of his firsthand experiences, he captured and maintained the rapt attention of us grandchildren, who sat wide-eyed, drinking in every word of one mind-boggling story after another. Accompanied by the subtlety of a raised eyebrow or a knowing smile, his tales transported our thoughts from our contemporary world to a bygone era that overflowed with romance and discovery.

One of our favorite stories was the one he told about the time he just happened to be high atop Kill Devil Hills in Kitty Hawk, North Carolina, on December 17, 1903, when two inventors named Orville and Wilbur Wright attempted to maneuver a home-built contraption from a standing position on the ground into the air.

As my grandfather described his view of the action, the brothers Wright were unsuccessful on their first attempts. For some reason or another, they thought that a tailwind takeoff was the proper procedure. They theorized, so he said, that with the air behind them, the craft would be more easily catapulted off the ground.

My grandfather—a young 12-year-old at the time—watched their futile attempts for more than a full hour. Finally he could remain quiet no longer. He shouted: "Why not take off *into* the wind for greater lift?"

At first they paid little attention to the youngster. But following a few more failures, Orville Wright suggested that they follow my grandfather's advice. They turned the *Flyer* around 180 degrees and, on their first attempt, got the aeroplane (as they called it) to rise eight feet off the ground and fly a grand total of 120 feet in 12 seconds.

As a crowning touch to his story, my grandfather would point upward. "So, because of my suggestion," he boldly proclaimed, "the first airplane, and every other airplane you see in the sky today, is able to fly."

Was my grandfather's story true? Official historical records of the event certainly don't confirm it. In fact, they never even hint that it could be true.

But to us grandkids, that really didn't matter. We enjoyed listening to the same story over and over again.

Most of the tales found in this book are 100 percent true. Others may be based on truth but are enhanced by exaggeration or an embellishment of one or more facts taken out of context. Some will raise more than the hint of a doubt. These disclaimers notwithstanding, all of these stories—some long, others short— are shared in order to give you a taste of what it's like to be a part of the family of aviation.

So, sit back, relax and enjoy. Let these *Tales from the Cockpit* bring you the unmatched joy akin to the priceless legacy given to those of us blessed with a grandfather named William Lyman Hall.

Part 1:

The Pioneers

"The Wright brothers created the single greatest cultural force since the invention of writing. The airplane became the first World Wide Web, bringing people, languages, ideas and values together."
— Bill Gates, CEO, Microsoft Corp.

Here's a tip of the pilot's hat to the pioneers of aviation—those men and women who dared to go where no person had traveled. Some were daredevils—wing walkers and aerobatic pilots—who became circus performers in front of jaw-dropped visitors to early air shows. Others were calculating academics who measured with precision the probabilities of a successful flight. For the most part they were ordinary men and women who envisioned life, both physically and emotionally, on a higher level. They refused to remain imprisoned by gravity. They dared to step out into unknown frontiers and pave the way for the rest of us.

To these brave souls, every pilot owes sincere thanks. These are some of their stories.

Planes, Trains and Flashlights

Prior to his famous flight from New York to Paris, Charles Augustus Lindbergh did whatever he could to earn a living. If a job required him to fly, so much the better. Therefore, on September 16, 1926, when the opportunity arose for him to deliver mail by air from St. Louis to Chicago, with a few stops in between, he leaped at the chance.

On this particular night, Lindbergh left St. Louis at about 4:45 p.m. and landed at Springfield, then at Peoria. Both airports, however, were out of fuel to sell, but Lindbergh figured he had more than enough to make it to Chicago.

An hour's delay by the local post office in Peoria in getting the mail to Lindbergh set him behind schedule, so much that the sun set behind him while he flew the final leg. The young pilot was still 50 miles from Chicago's Maywood Airport—his final destination.

Biplanes of that era were not equipped for night flying. In addition to the obvious hazards associated with flying in the dark, the pilot's only navigational aids were a hard-to-see compass (that required the help of a reliable flashlight) and as much of the scenery below as could be seen under the glow of the moon.

Adding to Lindbergh's woes that evening was the fact that a bank of fog reaching from the ground to about 600 feet had moved across the landscape, making it difficult, if not impossible, to discern what lay below.

Lindbergh used up a lot of extra time and fuel flying a zigzag pattern while sitting on his parachute (a "must" in this era of aviation) at an altitude of 1,000 feet in a vain attempt to find some familiar markings. He saw nothing except the ever-increasing fog. Because his plane was getting low on fuel, he moved his eyes from side to side as he searched for an open field that could serve as a temporary "airport."

He reached into his makeshift flight bag for a flare to light and drop to the ground with the hope that the light would penetrate enough of the fog to give him a picture of the surface. The flare failed to light.

Using dead reckoning, he continued to fly in what he believed to be the general direction of Maywood Airport. He saw a few miles ahead a dull glow in the fog, indicating that he was approaching a city. Hopefully it was Maywood.

He tossed out another flare. This one worked, but it only disappeared into the thick fog. Lindbergh prepared for the inevitable. He pulled back on the stick and took the plane to nearly 5,000 feet before the engine coughed and died from fuel starvation.

Lindbergh climbed out of the cockpit and, with one hand grasping a wing strut and the other holding his flashlight, stood on front edge of the left wing. After whispering a silent prayer, he leaped into the fog below. As soon as his parachute opened, he aimed his flashlight at the top of the fog, hoping to find a safe place to land.

His concentration on the layer of fog was interrupted when he heard the engine of his biplane fire up again. Apparently, when the airplane nosed down, some gasoline drained into the carburetor. Now Lindbergh envisioned a powered aircraft spiraling down toward him and his open chute. Imitating an Olympic swimmer, Lindbergh frantically clawed at the air in an attempt to move himself out of range of the attacking airplane. In his haste to get out of the way, he dropped his flashlight.

His efforts proved effective. He landed without a scratch in a cornfield that he could see only when he was 10 yards above the ground. The plane continued flying for two miles, then crashed in a nearby field but did not catch fire, thus allowing him to retrieve the mail for later delivery.

In his logbook, "Lucky Lindy" wrote: "The sheriff from Ottawa arrived, and we took the mail to be entrained at 3:30 a.m. for Chicago."

That train to Chicago never made it. It was derailed by a collision with a dead cow lying on the track. Local officials determined that foul play must have been involved. The cow, their investigation revealed, had been killed by a sharp blow to the head—from a falling flashlight.

Wilbur's Parrot Speech

Wilbur Wright may be one of the fathers of aviation. However, this rather modest inventor felt uneasy standing in front of an audience to give a speech. One of the few times he did speak, he left us with words that are often quoted. His remarks are, to this day, referred to as his "parrot speech."

On September 24, 1908, he agreed to be honored at a formal dinner hosted by the Aero-Club of Sarthe, France. He accepted on one condition—that he would not be required to give a formal speech.

Following a fine dinner and the presentation of a trophy honoring the first flight at Kitty Hawk, those in attendance clamored for Wright to speak to them. Wright yielded to their demands. He rose, stood behind the podium, and said, "I know of only one bird—the parrot—that talks, and it cannot fly very high or say very much."

With that, he sat down.

The Spruce Goose

William Lear, Jr., had a front-row seat to the aviation contributions of his father, who gave us the first popular private jet, in-car radios, and other inventions. As a bonus, young Bill got to meet some other trailblazers of aviation. He tells one such story in his popular book, *Fly Fast; Sin Boldly*:

"Early in 1947, when I was a mere lad of 18 years, I met with Howard Hughes for a private viewing of his controversial Hughes Hercules HK-1 flying boat (known today as the *Spruce Goose*), berthed at Long Beach Terminal Island in southern California. I was absolutely blown away by the fact that I would be shown the sacred innards of the pet project of the most famous (perhaps infamous) man in the aviation world.

"Mr. Hughes met Glenn Odekirk (an employee and close personal friend of Hughes), a couple of reporters from *Time* magazine who were writing a piece on the already legendary aircraft, and me at Mr. Hughes's Culver City Airport. We were early; he was right on time. He drove up in a plain vanilla Chevrolet. He stepped out, unshaven, wearing wrinkled khaki trousers, a white open-collared, rolled-up long-sleeved shirt, white tennis shoes, no socks, and his famous crumpled fedora. He was accompanied by a barefooted starlet—Jean Peters—whom he would later marry. Without taking time to introduce us to his companion, he led us to his converted B-25 bomber for a short flight to an airport near the location of his wooden wonder.

The Spruce Goose, *brainchild of the famous and eccentric Howard Hughes.*
Photo courtesy of Octave Chanute Aerospace Museum

"In my state of youthful admiration and wonderment I realized that this would be my sole opportunity to observe the 'Master' actually at the controls of an aircraft. I positioned myself in the rear cabin so as to be able to perceive Howard's every cockpit movement. He handled the controls with the confidence and smoothness of superb pilot, and this was after his near-fatal XF-11 crash in July of the previous year.

"Howard squeaked the plane onto an airstrip near Terminal Island. A bevy of cars whisked us to the *Goose's* protected dry-dock area at Pier E, Berth 21. Howard led us up a ramp and into the cavernous interior of this incredibly monstrous machine after requiring us to don slipper-socks over our shoes. He asked that we not gather together in any one location on the main cabin deck. It seems that the floor had a relatively low per-square-foot load limit. Too many folks standing in the wrong place could possibly result in one or more of our group dropping through the floor.

"Howard escorted us to the immense cockpit and briefed us on the technical aspects of this behemoth. The fuselage was 220 feet long, and the wingspan an astounding 320 feet, with a wing area of 11,430 square feet—a little more than a quarter of an acre.

"He then led us into the wing-root area, inside the main cabin, where there was access to each wing. At its root, each wing was 11 feet thick. You could actually walk out into the wings. With this advantage, a mechanic could service the engines during a flight.

"The airplane, built entirely of birch veneer (not spruce), had a gross weight of 400,000 pounds and was powered by eight Pratt & Whitney R4360 engines that developed 3,000hp each, for a grand total of an incredible 24,000hp.

"The airplane was built at the urging of the government during World War II. The feds signed a contract with

Mr. Hughes for a whopping $18 million to design and build the thing. When the war ended, the aircraft was still under construction. The government felt, therefore, that it was no longer needed and wanted to cancel the project. Hughes objected. He convinced Congress that he should be allowed to finish the project. He brazenly claimed that if his creation did not fly, he would leave the country.

"On the way back to our cars, I walked alongside Howard Hughes and stupidly asked if he really thought this huge bird would fly. He didn't reply. I then realized that he was becoming deaf. I repeated my question in a much louder voice. Without hesitation, he replied, 'Well, son, if it doesn't it'll sure be the fastest water taxi between here and Honolulu you ever saw!'

"The aircraft did, indeed, fly on November 2, 1947. But nobody knew about it ahead of time. With Hughes at the controls that day, the airplane taxied along the Long Beach Channel so that photographers could take pictures. To the surprise of everyone, at approximately 12:30 p.m., Hughes applied full power to the engines, pulled back on the yoke and lifted the *Goose* into the air. It flew for about 70 seconds over a span of one mile. Hughes then gently landed the fabric-covered flying boat into the water."

The *Spruce Goose* was never to fly again.

It now rests at the Evergreen Aviation Museum in McMinnville, Oregon.

Anne Morrow Lindbergh's First Flight

In December 1927, long before her marriage to the famed aviator, Anne Morrow Lindbergh and her family were offered a ride by her future husband in a Ford Tri-Motor. The following is her account of this, her first flight, originally published in *Bring Me a Unicorn*—a collection of her diaries and letters. Until her death in 2001 at the ripe old age of 94, Mrs. Lindbergh was a most positive ambassador for aviation. In her own words she describes her introduction to her newfound love of flight and her admiration of the man in the pilot's seat.

"Suddenly I felt the real sensation of going up—a great lift, like a bird, like one's dreams of flying—we soared in layers. That lift that took your breath away—there it was again! I had *real* and intense *consciousness* of flying. I was overjoyed. Then for the first time I looked down. We were high above fields, and there far, far below was a small shadow as of a great bird *tearing* along the neatly marked-off fields. It gave me the most tremendous shock to realize for the first time the terrific speed we were going at and that shadow meant *us*—*us* like a mirror! That 'bird'—it was *us*.

"We were over the city now; it looked like a child's model. The sun gleamed on the gold wings of that great statue in the square. How tiny it looked! The small drops of shadow circling the haystacks in the fields. The fields looked like braided cloth.

"He [Lindbergh] was so perfectly at home—all his movements mechanical. He sat easily and quietly, not rigidly, but

*An artist's rendering of the Ford Tri-Motor, in which Charles
Lindbergh took his future wife for her first airplane ride.
Print courtesy of Octave Chanute Aerospace Museum*

relaxed, yet alert. One hand on the wheel—one hand! He has the most tremendous hands. I can see him still, and the grasp, the strong wrist, the grip of the thumb, his other hand rubbing his nose. Looking clearly and calmly ahead, every movement quiet, ordered, easy—and *completely* harmonious. I don't know how I can say that, really, for he moved so very little and yet you felt the harmony of it.

"We were pointed towards the mountains. Oh, to go on and on—over the mountains! I could understand why people never can give it up.

"The sun on the tinsel wings of the matchstick statue, the minute circling cars—so small, so small—the tiny patch of green, the court of the Embassy, where we would have the garden party that afternoon and he would stand and shake hands with thousands of those black motes in the street.

"No wonder he has a disregard for death—and life. This is both.

"We were turning. In a minute we were wheeling around—'banking'—at a terrific angle, over on one wing. I did not look down until we were almost on the ground. I expected a terrific bounce. I looked out at the wheels; they grazed the ground, a cloud of dust but an imperceptible, balloon-like bounce, then again; we were down. We rolled in and stopped.

"We stepped out, dazed. I watched Colonel Lindbergh's head in the cockpit window, turning and looking out at the engine.

"It was a complex and intense experience. I will not be happy till it happens again."

"Blump!"

In 1927, one of the first pilots hired by the Pitcairn Mailwings, a mail-carrier service and a forerunner of Eastern Airlines, was a brash Texan named Amberse Banks. Banks was one of those so-called daredevil pilots who braved all kinds of weather in his biplane in order to get the mail through. On one evening, however, he nearly had a front-row seat to an aviation disaster.

Banks was flying his Pitcairn Orowing on a moonless night from Richmond, Virginia, to New York City. Directly ahead he spotted what appeared to be a large gray cloud. He was about to fly through it when one of those unique gut feelings known only to pilots told him something was wrong. At the last second he pulled back on the stick and zoomed over the "cloud," which suddenly lit up like a giant Christmas tree.

What Banks almost rammed was the United States Navy's giant dirigible, *Los Angeles*.

The Cigar Technique

Sometimes it's difficult for those of us who live in the 21st century to determine whether or not a story from the late 1920s is true. But, as Yogi Berra might say, "If it's not true, it should be."

One of those stories takes place in the days before VOR, LORAN or GPS, when mail-carrying pilots who flew bi-planes cross-country at night had virtually no aids to navigation. One innovative aviator allegedly used a device he called his "cigar technique." Just after the pilot took off from Cleveland, Ohio, he lit a specific brand of a tightly wrapped cigar. While flying above the night overcast, he waited until the cigar had burned down to one inch. At that precise moment, he would descend through the clouds and usually find Bellefontaine—his checkpoint. From there it was easy to find his designated airfield.

Willis Chase, of Newark, Ohio, is shown in this 1933 photo wearing the typical "uniform" for pilots. A helmet and goggles were optional.
Photo courtesy of the Willis Chase estate

The Rebel Genius

Howard Hughes, who was never shy about engaging in public debate with those in authority as to what could or could not be done, was also the world's poster child for recluses. After gaining international fame for his 1938 round-the-world flight, setting a speed record of three days, 19 hours, 14 minutes, he slowly drifted off into a cocoon-like existence. Even when the federal government commissioned him to build his famous *Spruce Goose*, the now billionaire focused his energies on projects to suit his own goals. According to most observers, he developed and honed a "Do It My Way or Else" attitude.

As owner of RKO Pictures, he produced classic movies such as *Scarface* and introduced a buxom Jane Russell to the public in *The Outlaw*—both of which challenged the standards imposed by Hollywood censors and other establishers of the nation's moral tone. Some associates claim that the chief motivating factor behind his creation of the *Goose* was to show his critics that his concept could, indeed, work.

One of the sad ironies in American history is that the man who delighted in pushing the envelopes of those who claimed something could not be done never left a detailed record of how he thought or the reasons behind his motivations. In 1971, a writer named Clifford Irving was paid a reported $750,000 for a manuscript he claimed was Hughes's autobiography. Hughes denied knowing anything about either the manuscript or Irving. The writer later confessed to the hoax and was sentenced to serve time in prison.

Look at What a 20-Dollar Flight Can Give You

Few people know that one of the great universities in America had its beginnings on a grass landing strip in Cincinnati, Ohio.

John Paul Riddle, less than 20 years after the Wright brothers flew their *Flyer* on its maiden voyage at Kitty Hawk, North Carolina, was one of an idolized group of daredevils known as barnstormers. This native of Pikeville, Kentucky, had purchased a used Jenny aircraft for $250 and, later, a more sophisticated Hisso Standard and gave rides at county fairs and other celebrations to those who wanted to experience the thrill of flight.

"On weekends, I took off from Kelly Field in Cincinnati to small towns around Ohio and Indiana. I charged a person ten dollars for a short ride around the countryside. Sometimes pretty girls flew for free," he admits.

Approaching Riddle one day was a rather wealthy businessman by the name of T. Higbee Embry.

"How much for a ride?" asked Embry.

"How much you got with you?" responded Riddle.

"Uh... twenty dollars."

"That's exactly the price. Hop in," said Riddle.

Thus began a close friendship that led to a partnership, the joint ownership of the first distributorship for Waco Aircraft, and an aviation school at which students could learn, in a systematic way, how to fly safely.

Two Curtiss JN-4s, or "Jennys," fly over the countryside in the early days of aviation.
Photo courtesy of Octave Chanute Aerospace Museum

This modest union became the basis for the Embry-Riddle Company that later developed into the internationally famous Embry-Riddle Aeronautical University, with campuses in Daytona Beach, Florida, in Prescott, Arizona, and at hundreds of military bases throughout the world.

Trailblazing Women

Ten-year-old Florence Shusty, of Connellsville, Pennsylvania, sat at the family dinner table one night and proudly announced to her family that, when she grew up, she was going to fly airplanes.

"My parents laughed," she recalls, "but I didn't."

Fifteen years later, the spunky blonde not only became the first woman ever to earn a pilot's license at her local airport, but she also joined the first-ever group of women military aviators for the United States, known as the Women Airforce Service Pilots (WASP).

During World War II, women of the WASP were not permitted to fly combat in either the Atlantic or Pacific theaters. Instead, they flew the United States, ferrying aircraft, towing targets, testing repaired planes and, yes, even teaching male cadets. They flew everything from a two-place, biwing Stearman trainer to a four-engine B-29 Super Fortress bomber.

Although they remained stateside, their work was not without danger. Within two years, 18 of Shusty's comrades were killed and many more were injured. "They didn't bring in psychiatrists for us. They cleaned up, you grabbed your chute and you went on with it. We had a camaraderie and a purpose. That kept us going.

"Glamour? Hell, it was hard work," says the feisty Shusty. The hardest part of the job, she says, was overcoming the resentment by the male pilots in what was known as

Women of the WASP flew all kinds of aircraft, including the PT-13 Stearman.
Photo courtesy of Octave Chanute Aerospace Museum

the Army Air Corps. "As one of my check-ride instructors told me, 'I don't like women and I *especially* don't like women pilots.' Each of us women had to prove ourselves on every flight."

In spite of the WASP's success, male civilian pilots and flight instructors who didn't want to be drafted mounted an anti-WASP campaign, arguing that women were taking their jobs. Their rhetoric worked. By the end of 1944, the WASP was demobilized and the women were sent home. "I felt like an old piece of garbage that was thrown away," she said. "At least for the time being, the military forgot women had ever been in the cockpit."

It wasn't until 1977 that WASP veterans persuaded Congress to recognize their war service and grant them military status and benefits.

Florence Shusty married one year following the war and retired from flying until her husband's death in 1988. Today she travels the country giving speeches about the WASP. She and her former colleagues still keep in touch. "Our ranks are getting thin," she said, noting that only about 540 of the original WASP are still alive. "We did a good job, and we'd like people to catch us now while they can still hear about what we did."

Early Glide Slope

J. Paul Riddle, one of the founders of the company that eventually developed into Embry-Riddle Aeronautical University, loved to tell stories about the early days of barnstorming and of the pioneers who transported the mail via biplanes cross country.

Pilots of that era did not have radar following or sophisticated instrumentation to guide them through the soup. As a result, when flying into an airport during the days when visibility was less than a mile, airmen were forced to use rather crude navigational aids.

Using certain familiar landmarks, a pilot could determine if he was in the general vicinity of the airport of destination. But could he make a proper approach for a landing? One of the ways a pilot could know that he was lined up with a runway in a rural area was to fly approximately 100 feet above the ground and watch the cattle below. If the cattle were calm and stood still, that meant they were used to the roar of an airplane engine. If the cattle became nervous and started to scatter, the pilot knew he was not on the right track to the runway. He would then execute a go-around and try again, looking for the more contented cows in the area.

"Lucky Lindy"

Nearly every fan of aviation knows the story of how Captain (he would later become a colonel, then a brigadier general) Charles Lindbergh piloted his aircraft—*The Spirit of St. Louis*—across the Atlantic Ocean. What most people do not know was that he was not the *first* person to fly across that ocean. In truth, he was the 92nd. His flight differed from those who went before him for two reasons:

1) It was a non-stop flight between two cities;
2) It was made solo.

Eight years earlier, a wealthy New York hotel owner—Raymond Orteig—offered a prize of $25,000 to anyone who would fly non-stop from New York to Paris. A few brave pilots attempted the feat. They all failed; some, unfortunately, were killed.

What many people may not know is that when "Lucky Lindy" (a name he hated, because, as he said, "There was no luck involved; it was the result of hard training") took off from Roosevelt Field in Nassau County near New York City in the early morning hours on May 20, 1927, Lindbergh had had no sleep whatsoever the night before. Because he could not sleep, Lindbergh got out of bed and was at the airport at 2:15 a.m.

During the hours before his flight, Lindbergh made certain that his plane was filled with 451 gallons of fuel and that his "in-flight meals" of four sandwiches and two canteens of water were in the one seat. He also took time to evaluate the weather reports. They were not encouraging. The forecast was for rain and fog along his proposed northeastern flight path.

After his crew arrived at the airfield, Lindbergh climbed into the *Spirit* and fired up the engine at 7:40 a.m. At 7:52, the wheels of the heavily loaded, silver, fabric-covered airplane with the designation N-X-211 rolled and bounced over the rain-soaked field. Lindbergh pulled back on the stick and got the plane airborne. He missed by only 20 feet hitting telegraph wires near the end of the runway.

Within the first hour of flight, the excitement of the morning and the lack of sleep combined to take their toll. Lindbergh grew weary. Traveling at an average speed of 107.9 mph, with engine rpm indicating 1,750, Lindbergh's energy was sapped as he maneuvered through a violent storm near Nova Scotia. On this moonless night, the plane headed over the dark ocean.

He had had no sleep for 36 hours and had at least 24 more to go. He later wrote in his diary: "The worst part about fighting sleep is that the harder you fight, the more you strengthen your enemy and weaken your resistance to him."

Once he awoke at the last minute as the aircraft fell off onto one wing. Twice he suddenly found himself in a spiral toward the waves and had to right the plane less than 100 feet above the water.

After he climbed back to 10,000 feet, Lindbergh detected ice that began to build up on the wings. He was forced to fly at a much lower altitude than planned in order to stay in warmer temperatures.

During his 14th hour into the flight, Lindbergh entertained serious thoughts about returning to the United States. He dismissed that idea. Instead, he kept chanting to himself: "There's no alternative but death and failure."

His need for sleep continually increased. At times he had to use his fingers to prop his eyes open.

Sometimes, he admitted later, he slept even with his eyes open. Once he was awakened by the sound of the waves roaring just ten feet below him. After 28 hours he finally spotted land. Twenty minutes later he was flying over the rugged coastline of Ireland. Miraculously, in spite of severe winds and several bouts with fatigue, he was only three miles off course.

Energy surged into his body. For the final six hours he had no problem staying awake.

Shortly before 10 p.m., he spotted Le Bourget. He circled the Eiffel Tower at 4,000 feet, then landed without incident... until, that is, tens of thousands of cheering Frenchmen surged past security and rushed his plane. As soon as Lindbergh shut down the engine of the *Spirit* and opened the side door, he was hoisted onto the shoulders of some of the people and carried to the terminal.

What followed that evening was the most welcomed and best deserved sleep of his young life.

******

"I was astonished at the effect my successful landing in France had on the nations of the world. To me, it was like a match lighting a bonfire."

—Charles A. Lindbergh

Moving Mecca

On May 19, 1997, a monument was dedicated near the runway of Roosevelt Field in Nassau County, New York, to mark the spot where Charles A. Lindbergh had set off for his historic solo flight across the Atlantic Ocean to Paris 70 years earlier. There's only one problem with the monument. Lindbergh never took off from the spot. In fact, he never took off from this airfield.

The airport, known today as Roosevelt Field, was actually another airport back in 1927 called Curtiss Field. According to Josh Stoff, curator of Nassau's Cradle of Aviation Museum, two years following Lindbergh's heroic flight, the people who owned Roosevelt Field bought Curtiss Field and renamed the entire site Roosevelt Field.

If that monument were placed at the exact spot of Lindbergh's initial roll-out, it would have to be near the checkout counter at Bob's Grocery Store, located at the Roosevelt Field Shopping Center that was built on the site of the old Roosevelt Field. For those who are interested in more historic details, the *Spirit of St. Louis* would have continued its roll past Marshall's and lifted off somewhere between the garage at Fourtunoff and the back entrance to Cozymel's Restaurant.

As to the exact spot where Lindbergh landed, however, there is absolutely no confusion. At last report, Paris and Le Bourget Field still remain in the same locations they were back in 1927.

Part 2:

When Airplanes Went to War

"Never in the field of human conflict was so much owed by so many to so few."

—Winston Churchill, 1940, about
the Royal Air Force in World War II

August 6, 1945

One of the most memorable dates of World War II was August 6, 1945—the day of the first explosion of the atomic bomb on the callow city of Hiroshima, Japan. The bomb was dropped during the early morning hours from a B-29 named *Enola Gay*. Its pilot was Colonel Paul Warfield Tibbets.

Tibbets eventually retired from the U.S. Air Force as a brigadier general in 1966, following 29 and a half years of service. During his military career, he received many distinguishing awards, including the Purple Heart, Distinguished Service Cross and Distinguished Flying Cross.

In civilian life he became a respected businessman, rising to the rank of CEO of Executive Jet Aircraft (now NetJet). His biography has been well documented on television specials and in his book, *The Tibbets Story*.

Today, while dividing time between homes in Ohio and Florida, Gen. Tibbets is a popular speaker at banquets and other gatherings of pilots and World War II buffs.

In his own words, this is the story of his fateful flight on August 6, 1945:

"I kept telling myself: 'Paul, take it easy. This is just another takeoff. You've done this many times before.' But my shaking hands that gripped the controls of the B-29 'Super Fortress' belied any futile attempt to calm my nerves.

"I slowly pushed forward the throttles of the bomber recently named *Enola Gay* (after my mother). Just two hours earlier, the plane was topped off with enough fuel for a 17-hour round-trip flight. The weight of two extra crew members that brought the total to 12, plus some extra baggage— a rather ugly, gunmetal-painted 9,000 pounds of explosive power in one casing dubbed 'Little Boy'—forced the shiny aluminum-covered aircraft to test its ability as never before.

"The propellers of the four 2,200hp Wright Cyclone engines churned faster. The plane inched its way forward down the 11,000-foot runway on Tinian Island in the South Pacific. My copilot, Capt. Robert Lewis, called out the airspeeds: 'We're at 75 miles per hour... 80... 90... 105... .' He kept one eye on the instrument panel and the other on the fast-approaching end of the runway.

"I pushed the wheel forward a bit to keep the plane on the ground. I always liked to reach 10 to 12 miles per hour faster than normal takeoff speed as an extra 'insurance' against a premature stall.

"'More than 120...140... ' barked Bob Lewis. His voice grew louder as we neared the end of the runway. 'You can rotate any time now!' he shouted.

"At precisely 2:45 a.m., when the plane was only 100 feet from the end of the runway and the airspeed indicator reached 155, I eased back the yoke. The plane lunged skyward and headed smoothly toward our initial altitude of 5,000 feet. During this phase of the flight, Capt. Derek Parsons would 'load' the bomb—a precautionary strategy in the event the plane were to crash on takeoff and cause a devastating explosion.

"On the day before this flight, a number of our guys signed the casing, which measured 28 inches in diameter and 12 feet long. Still, most of our crew remained uncertain as to what we were about to do. Rumors of an 'atomic something-or-other' had circulated for months among the men of the 509th Composite Group Headquarters where we were stationed. Only a few of us knew exactly what to expect— at least we *thought* we knew what to expect.

"One of the reasons for the secrecy of our mission was the skepticism shared by some of the principals involved. Admiral W. D. Leahy, President Franklin Roosevelt's military advisor, for example, was convinced the bomb would not explode. I was determined to prove him wrong.

"We set a northwest course for Japan and headed toward one of three cities—Nagasaki, Kokura, or our primary target, Hiroshima. Weather conditions and visibility would dictate which city would be a name destined to appear in history books.

"The fact that we were carrying a bomb with the explosive power of 20,000 tons of TNT should have been mind-boggling, I suppose. On top of this, I was not 100-percent sure that we would be able to complete our mission. Many things could go wrong. Of course, I did not allow myself to convey that fear to any of the other crew.

"Perhaps my relative calmness lay in the fact that I was too young to appreciate the potential perils of the mission. Yet, at age 29, I was considered 'the old man' by the remainder of the flight crew. Although most of the war movies back home saw the war fought by men the age of John Wayne, in the 'real war,' the task of directing a Super Fortress on any mission was entrusted to kids just out of high school or college. We just had to grow up—fast.

"I set the autopilot before I walked to the back of the plane to reassure all the men that everything was going as planned. Capt. Parsons assured me that the bomb was engaged. I nodded. 'Hope we won't need these,' I said as I patted a small pillbox in my shirt pocket. The box contained 12 cyanide capsules—one for each member of the crew—in the event that we were shot down. We did not want to chance being captured and forced to reveal any secrets of the weapon. Capt. Parsons and I were the only two aboard the plane who knew about this alternative plan for suicide.

"Once I knew that the bomb was engaged, I returned to my seat in the cockpit and took the airplane to 9,300 feet—its cruising altitude.

"The hours passed slowly. The hypnotic droning of the engines added to the weariness created by the anxieties of the moment and my lack of sleep over the past 48 hours. Bob Lewis took control of the plane while I took a brief catnap.

"After six hours of flying, we approached the shores of Iwo Jima—an infamous eight square miles of real estate on which thousands of brave Americans had lost their lives just a few months earlier.

"Weather planes had been sent ahead of us. They reported that conditions were favorable for Hiroshima—a city relatively untouched by previous bombing raids.

"At 7:30 a.m., Capt. Parsons made some last-minute adjustments to ensure the bomb's accuracy. He notified us that all was now ready.

"Our ground speed was 330 mph. We set our course at 264 degrees. We were now less than two hours away.

"We climbed to 30,700 feet—our bombing altitude. Bob Lewis and I scanned the landscape below. Our flight maps were excellent—showing all of the essential landmarks. When we spotted a unique 'T-shaped' bridge, we knew we were just minutes away from our target.

"Two other planes followed us. *The Great Artiste* would drop recording devices to measure the impact of the bomb; another plane, loaded with photography equipment to record the event, lagged far enough behind to remain out of danger.

"I told our crew that we would soon be over Hiroshima. Maj. Thomas Ferebee was a seasoned expert at dropping bombs. I believe he could actually thread a needle from 30,000 feet. He told me he was ready and that the target was in sight.

"'It's all yours,' I said.

"I expected some ack-ack fire from the ground, but there was none. I guess their weapons were ineffective against aircraft at our altitude.

"At 9:14 and 17 seconds a.m., Ferebee flicked a toggle switch that set off a high-pitched tone. Exactly one minute later, the tone ceased, the bomb-bay doors opened automatically, and 'Little Boy' tumbled out toward the awakening city below. The aircraft quickly hopped upward at the sudden loss of 9,000 pounds.

"We had traveled over 2,000 miles and were only 17 seconds off schedule.

"Immediately we banked 155 degrees to our right at a sharp, 60-degree angle. The *Enola Gay* appeared to groan under the pressure of being flown like a fighter plane. Our tail gunner, SSgt. Robert Caron, compared his experience to that of a schoolboy at the end of a group of classmates as they played crack the whip.

"Bob Lewis and I covered our eyes with sunglasses that had been issued to all the crew, but they made it impossible to see the instrument panel. We slipped them back onto our caps.

"It took 43 seconds for the bomb to drop and reach its explosion altitude of 1,890 feet above the surface. Although we were 10 and a half miles from the explosion and were looking away, we were temporarily blinded by a flash of light that filled the sky. Our vision returned in just a few seconds. We saw below a huge fireball, resembling a thousand suns.

"Bob Caron, the only man to see the entire picture, reported a shockwave approaching us at about the speed of sound—1,100 feet per second. We braced ourselves. The wave hit us with a force two and a half times that of gravity. Bob Lewis described this by saying it was as if some giant had struck the plane with a large telephone pole.

"A huge, purple mushroom loomed upward to 45,000 feet—three miles higher than we were flying. The ground was ablaze with fire and bubbling tar. We watched in stunned silence.

"Bob Lewis said I whispered, 'My God.' If I did, it was a prayer, not a curse.

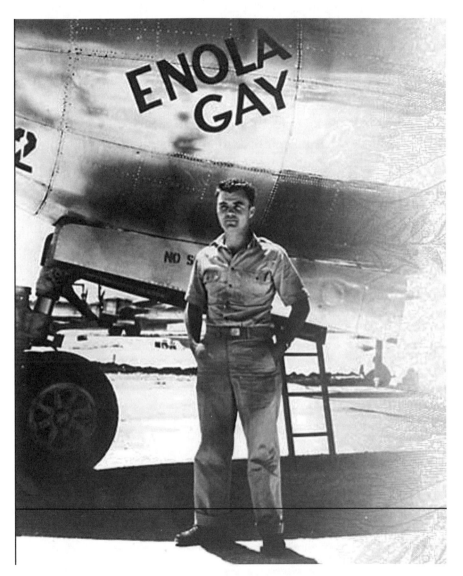

Colonel Paul Tibbets by his B-29 bomber, the Enola Gay. *The colonel, his crew, and their airplane helped change the course of WWII and of history.*

"I pointed the plane southeast toward our base. We could see the mushroom cloud linger over the city until we got 400 miles away from the target. I reached inside my flight jacket, pulled out my favorite pipe, lit it, leaned back and puffed away. For the first time in eight hours, I felt relief.

"After the development of the photographs we learned exactly how much damage the bomb had inflicted—four and a half square miles of the city had melted and literally vanished. An estimated 85,000 men, women and children were killed instantly; more would later die from the effects of radiation. The Japanese government, nevertheless, refused to surrender. Not until another atomic bomb was dropped on Nagasaki three days later did the nation's leaders finally decide to give up.

"On August 6, 1945, we who were aboard the *Enola Gay* knew in our hearts that the war was already over. We also knew something else: from this day forward, the world would never be the same."

Perils of Flying a Messerschmitt

The following story is 100-percent true. The actual name of the pilot, however, has been changed at his request, since he is a naturalized American citizen and, for personal reasons, wishes to remain aloof from his firsthand experiences with Germany's participation in World War II.

Hilmar Schmidt was born in Leipzig, Germany in 1927. Following the outbreak of World War II, not surprisingly, he was drafted into the military. High marks in school and his obvious superior intelligence identified him as a prime candidate to fly for the *Luftwaffe*.

Following the end of the war in 1945, Schmidt attended college in Germany and in America, then was accepted into Concordia Lutheran Seminary in St. Louis, where he studied theology. After serving as a pastor for a small congregation in Illinois, he earned his Ph.D. in theology from the University of Chicago and served as a respected professor at a variety of universities and seminaries. He is the author of seven published books on biblical theology.

This is his story of one of his training flights that shows some of the frustration of the times:

"I was, like every other teenager in Germany, drafted into the military on my 17th birthday. I had dreamed of flying ever since I was old enough to look at the sky and discern that airplanes made it possible to escape the force of gravity that entrapped most everyone else on this planet. I also convinced myself that speed is life. Even though the war was drawing to a close and I knew deep in my heart that we had slim hopes of winning, I was extremely pleased when told that I would become a pilot for my country during the most perilous time in its history.

"I was trained in the famous Messerschmitt BF109-G. We new flyers were not allowed to fly the newer 109-K models, so we got the leftovers. Yet no matter what model of Messerschmitt you flew in those days, it was still a dangerous airplane.

"Today, there is some romance associated with the Messerschmitt; a remarkable 2,000hp Daimler Benz engine provided it with a maximum speed of 450 mph. It was noted and feared, I suppose, for its diving attacks from high altitudes. But in all reality it was a miserable plane to land or taxi. With its limited visibility, it did not provide the pilot a good view of an approaching runway. The landing gear that came out of the fuselage, not out of the wings, was far too narrow; it caused many of these planes during a crosswind landing to tip on their wings. The 80-pound canopy was constructed with hinges on the left side; in the event you opened it while taxiing too quickly, a gust of wind could actually topple the aircraft.

"I was able to solo after only five hours of training. That was because the Germans needed to get as many airplanes into the air as possible in a short time. My first 50 hours or so were uneventful. I had no air-to-air combat. The most 'action' I saw was serving as an escort during one bombing raid.

"Following one rather routine flight, I was returning to my base in the *Luftgau*, our training area. A headwind of 25 knots caused me to report later than scheduled. It also resulted in a flashing red warning light on the panel, indicating that I was getting low on fuel. I breathed a sigh of relief when I spotted my airport just five miles ahead. As a training field, it wasn't the best; bombing raids left this field—as they did so many others—with only one active runway. In all reality, due to the potholes and cracked cement, that runway would have been closed in nearly any other circumstance.

"As I approached for landing, the tower operator advised me that I would go around, because an airplane was still on the runway—another victim of that lousy landing gear configuration. While the red light continued to flash, I made a 360-degree turn around the airport. As I lined up the airplane for my final approach, I was advised by the tower that the runway was still not clear. 'Go around,' demanded the operator.

"I told him that I could possibly do this only one more time, since I was very low on gasoline. After circling the field one more time and the red light now glowing steadily, I knew this would be my last opportunity to land with power. But while I was on final approach, I was told, once again, that the runway was closed.

"I had no alternative but to land the airplane to the side of the runway. So I guided it as best I could toward a long strip of grass that paralleled the runway. I wasn't frightened, probably because I was too young to appreciate the potential danger. I aimed the airplane for the grass and, to my amazement, was able to set the plane down quite easily. The only problem was that in all this confusion I failed to lower the landing gear.

"The airplane settled on its belly and bent the prop, but I was able to climb out of the cockpit quickly to avoid a possible fire.

"Several of my comrades, along with my commanding officer, saw the entire thing. They ran from the barracks toward me and my now crippled 109-G.

"'Are you all right?' they asked.

"I assured them I was.

"'What went wrong?' asked my commanding officer.

"I knew I would be in trouble if I told them what I did, so I lied. 'The gear would not go down,' I said.

"Within a few minutes, mechanics had arrived at the scene and, in front of us all, jacked up the airplane. The wheels came out of the undercarriage easily with a decisive *PLOP!*

"That's when they shipped me off to the damn infantry."

*The army's first airplane was a Wright Type B, accepted at Fort Meyer,
Va., in 1909 and now in the Smithsonian. Lieutenants Lahm and
Foulis, the army's first pilots, received instruction in this airplane.
Photo courtesy of Octave Chanute Aerospace Museum*

"So it was that the war in the air began. Men rode upon the whirlwind that night and slew and fell like archangels. The sky rained heroes upon the astonished earth. Surely the last fights of mankind were the best. What was the heavy pounding of your Homeric swordsmen, what was the creaking charge of chariots, besides this swift rush, this crash, this giddy triumph, this headlong sweep to death?"

—H. G. Wells, from *The World Set Free*, 1914

******

"There is a peculiar gratification on receiving congratulations from one's squadron for a victory in the air. It is worth more to be a pilot than the applause of the whole outside world. It means that one has won the confidence of men who share the misgivings, the aspirations, the trials and the dangers of aeroplane fighting.

"However, I have yet to find one single individual who has attained conspicuous success in bringing down enemy aeroplanes who can be said to be spoiled either by his successes or by the generous congratulations of his comrades. If he were capable of being spoiled he would not have had the character to have won continuous victories, for the smallest amount of vanity is fatal in aeroplane fighting. Self-distrust rather is the quality to which many a pilot owes his protracted existence."

—Eddie Rickenbacker, from *Fighting the Flying Circus*

Sage Advice from the "Red Baron"

One of the complaints by the German troops during the first World War was the repeated strafing of fields in which they were mired by pilots of their own side. Perhaps this action by pilots of the biplanes was due to their desire to practice flying maneuvers. The field infantry often regarded these runs as mere attempts to show off.

In his attempt to thwart this display of aeronautical prowess, the respected ace known around the world as "The Red Baron" issued this blistering verbal attack in 1917: "The duty of the fighter pilot is to patrol his area of the sky and shoot down any enemy fighters in that area. Anything else is rubbish."

He is credited with shooting down 80 enemy aircraft.

Baron Manfred von Richtofen, the "Red Baron"
AP/WWP

"Months of preparation, one of those few opportunities, and the judgment of a split-second are what makes one pilot an ace, while others think back on what they could have done."
—Col. Gregory "Pappy" Boyington, USMC, legendary leader of the "Black Sheep Squadron"

******

Empire of the Son

Another example of how difficult it is to discern whether or not tales from the cockpits are 100-percent true is the classic story of Lt. Cdr. Edward Henry "Butch" O'Hare. This legendary airman received the Congressional Medal of Honor for his actions against the Japanese during the early part of World War II and defending the U.S.S. *Lexington*.

According to official government records, the young graduate of the U.S. Naval Academy had taken off from the carrier only to realize he was low on fuel. His flight leader ordered him to return to his mother ship to refuel. A few miles away from his carrier, O'Hare spotted a squadron of Japanese Zeroes heading toward the fleet to attack. With all its fighter planes gone, the carrier was virtually defenseless. Single-handedly, he dove into the formation of planes and attacked. He shot at them until all of his ammunition had run out and knocked six enemy planes out of the air. Then, O'Hare, in a last desperate bid to protect the carrier, dove at the remaining planes in an attempt to clip off a wing, a tail, or anything else that would disable another Zero.

Finally, the remainder of his squadron responded to calls from the carrier. The sight of the extra fighters caused the Japanese squadron to take off in another direction. Butch O'Hare and his fighter, both badly shot up, limped back to the carrier.

Films from the camera that was rigged in the nose of O'Hare's airplane showed the extent to which he went to protect his fleet. For this, President Franklin Roosevelt bestowed upon him the military's highest honor.

In November 1943, O'Hare was killed over the Pacific in another combat with the Japanese. His body was never found.

Today, most Americans know his name, because Chicago's O'Hare Airport (previously called Orchard Depot) is named in his honor.

A parallel story involved another Chi-Town celebrity (in the broadest sense of the word). It deals with an educated mobster known as "Easy Eddie." Eddie was the lawyer for the notorious Al Capone during the heyday of the "Roaring '20s." Eddie was instrumental in assisting Capone in a variety of unethical and illegal schemes. Although he probably never pulled a trigger, he was keenly aware of Capone's personal logbook of slaughter of other gang members and innocent citizens.

Following years of association with the underworld, Easy Eddie did a 180-degree turn. He provided the necessary information to the FBI and other authorities that eventually sent Al Capone to prison for income tax evasion.

Why did Easy Eddie turn state's evidence? That depends on whom you believe. Since Eddie had a son, some speculate that he wanted to leave his son a legacy of which he could be proud; he wanted his son to teach his son about integrity. Others say he could see the handwriting on the wall; he believed Capone would be caught eventually, and if he cooperated with the feds he might avoid imprisonment himself and secure an appointment to the Naval Academy at Annapolis for his son (even if it would be at the expense of a more worthy candidate).

Following Capone's capture, Eddie was gunned down by what is believed to have been some of Capone's henchmen who were angry at his unfaithfulness to their boss.

There is, of course, a connection between the two stories. Easy Eddie's son was called "Butch"—the same Butch O'Hare who became a war hero and after whom one of the world's biggest airport is named.

That part of the story, at least, is true.

*An artist's rendering of the Boeing B-17 Flying Fortress, an
integral part of the Allied victory in Europe in WWII.
Print courtesy of Octave Chanute Aeropace Museum*

******

*"Anybody who doesn't have fear is an idiot.   It's just that
you must make the fear work for you.   Hell, when somebody
shot at me, it made me madder than hell, and all I wanted to
do was shoot back."*

—Brig. Gen. Robin Olds

The Original Raiders

Much has been written about one of the first heroes of America's involvement in World War II—General Jimmy Doolittle. Through fascinating books such as *The First Heroes* written by Craig Nelson, we become increasingly more amazed at the bravery of those who literally plunged themselves into unknown territory.

The 16 B-25 aircraft and the 80 men assigned to carrying out the first raid on Japan on April 18, 1942, met one unexpected obstacle after another.

The initial plan was for the aircraft to launch from carriers approximately 450 miles from land, to hit Japan at dusk, then retreat to China—630 miles away. However, because the carriers were spotted by a spy ship earlier than expected, the planes had to take off 650 miles from the Japanese coast.

The pilots knew that they did not carry enough fuel aboard their airplanes to complete the mission, but they left anyway.

Along the way, other Japanese lookouts spotted the aircraft but paid no attention to them. It was much akin to the situation of those who reported airplanes approaching Pearl Harbor four months earlier. The Japanese were extremely confident that the enemy was not equipped to invade their soil.

The 16 aircraft dropped bombs on Tokyo, then took off for China.

A B-25 bomber is shown here with its successful bomb runs represented on the fuselage.
Photo courtesy of Octave Chanute Aerospace Museum

The Americans suffered little damage. Only one airplane was shot up, but not enough to prevent it from flying.

The physical damage to Tokyo was not horrific. Approximately 50 of the enemy were killed—some from bombs from the Americans, others from the shells fired from anti-aircraft guns of the Japanese. But the psychological damage was the most profound. Much like that inflicted on America as a result of Pearl Harbor, both military and civilians of Japan now realized that they could actually lose the war.

Even more importantly, it proved to Americans two other truths. The raid demonstrated that air power was a vital factor in war. It also showed Americans back home that they could win the war.

The Raid's Aftermath

As expected, the aircraft ran out of fuel far short of their intended landing target in China. Instead, when the engines began to sputter, the airmen bailed out of their craft into the dark of the night.

Two factors gave them extra doses of anxiety. First, in the moonless night, they knew not what lay beneath them. Second, none had ever parachuted before. This was the first solo jump for all 80 men.

As it turned out, they landed in China, but it was a Japanese-controlled section of the country.

What happened to the downed crew is akin to Paul Harvey's "The Rest of the Story."

Eight were captured and spent 40 arduous months in a Japanese prison camp. One went insane. Two were beaten to death. One was starved to death. One kept his mind focused on Christ's crucifixion and said to himself: *If Jesus could forgive his torturers while enduring this, I can forgive my jailers.* His name was Jacob DeShazer—a bombardier on one of the B-25s.

In 1948, he was sent by the Free Methodist Church back to Japan as a missionary. There he met a former Japanese pilot—Mitsuo Fuchida—who became a Christian. Mitsuo Fuchida just happened to be the man who led the raid for the Japanese on Pearl Harbor.

And Yet One More PS

On that mission, 50 percent of the 20- to 24-year-old men were gung-ho, akin to Notre Dame football players running onto the field before a big game. The other 50 percent were certain that this would be the last day of their lives. Those who had the latter feeling later confessed that when the bombing began, they were no longer afraid. Instead, they felt a strange calm come over them; all they focused on was doing a good job.

As a lasting tribute to his brave men, when General Doolittle was given the Congressional Medal of Honor by President Franklin Roosevelt, he refused to accept it unless he took it in the name of all 80 men who flew on that mission.

The president willingly granted his request.

Even a War Needs a Happy Hour

Dr. Robert Chilcoat of Sommerset, New Jersey, loves to tell stories about his father, Capt. Jess Chilcoat, Jr., who was a B-25 pilot for the Army Air Corps during World War II. One of the favorites he liked to repeat was the time his dad was an instructor at a local air base in Bakersfield, California.

One morning, so the story goes, his base commander called him into his office and shut the door. "Captain," he says, "we have a serious problem over at the Officers' Club."

"Oh?" responded Capt. Chilcoat. "What's that, sir?"

"We're almost out of whiskey," said the CO, "and I can't get any more for at least a month."

The captain knew this was serious business.

"What can I do to help?"

"I want you to select a crew you can trust, draw enough money from the bursar, and fly that B-25 of yours up to Canada and fill it with booze." The CO filled out the papers giving authorization for the flight.

"This mission is top secret," he continued. "You are to tell no one where you're going. You are to return here tomorrow night, taxi to the far end of the field, and wait while a crew comes out to unload you. No one must ever know about this. Is that clear?"

"Uh... isn't that illegal, sir?" asked the captain.

"There's a war going on, Captain," snapped the CO. "And sometimes we have to bend the rules. I will tell you this. If anything goes wrong, you are completely on your own. I will deny any knowledge of this mission. Is that clear?"

"Yessir," said Captain Chilcoat.

Chilcoat grabbed his best friend and a couple of others he thought he could trust and headed for Canada in the B-25. They landed at a small strip near a moderate-sized town in British Columbia, figuring to avoid big cities such as Vancouver, but to find a town that was large enough to have some good-sized liquor stores.

After persuading a fixed base operator to drive them into town in a pickup truck, they went to a local store and bought 50 cases of whiskey—a hefty order, indeed. They were certain they would be questioned by the Royal Canadian Mounted Police.

When they returned to the airport, they decided that the safest place to load the cases and maintain the proper weight and balance would be in the bomb bay doors.

On the way back to Bakersfield, Chilcoat and his crew prayed that the bomb bay doors would not let go and drop the cases of whiskey over some unsuspecting field. Lest the bottles break, Chilcoat made the smoothest, gentlest landing of his career at the Bakersfield airstrip.

Morale at the Officers' Club stayed high, and we won the war. The only fallout from the entire mission was a few days later when one of the maintenance crew was found drunk on duty behind a hangar with half a bottle of Canadian Club in his hand. He claimed he'd found it in a B-25.

No one believed him.

A B-25 with an inspiring recruiting message on its fuselage.
Photo courtesy of Octave Chanute Aerospace Museum

Part 3:

The Presidents

"I have the greatest job in the world. I get to fly the Sacred Cow."

> —Unidentified pilot of the C-87, airplane
> for President Franklin D. Roosevelt

The Sacred Cow

Quite possibly the most famous airplane in the world today is *Air Force One*. The "Flying White House" has transported America's Chief Executive on his travels from 1944 to the present day.

Today's presidential airplane is a sleek 747 that contains all the gadgets and gizmos of the finest corporate office, plus the technology that allows the President of the United States to communicate with any world leader.

What we know today as *Air Force One* was not met with overwhelming approval at its inception. Franklin Delano Roosevelt was the first of our presidents who traveled by air. His plane was the result of a contract signed between the

Army Air Corps and the Consolidated-Vultee Corporation that involved the conversion of a C-87 into a traveling Oval Office. Baptized *Guess Where II*, the plane had several unique features, not the least of which was the first elevator ever installed in an airplane fuselage. This enabled President Roosevelt to enter and exit on his wheelchair with greater ease.

Later the airplane—officially known as "Aircraft 42-107451" (the assigned serial number as painted on its tail) or *The Flying White House*—was dubbed by presidential advisor and close friend Bernard Baruch as *The Sacred Cow*. Reporters loved the term and, among themselves, used it freely. Legend has it that even FDR accepted the title.

In spite of his eagerness to fly, President Roosevelt seldom used the aircraft known as *The Sacred Cow*. Many of his aides expressed fear of what might happen in the event of a fire.

Their concern was not without justification. If, indeed, history is the best predictor of the future, the book on the C-87 could have been written on asbestos. The record of the airplane included an extraordinary number of in-flight fires.

Part of the reason for this malfunction was that the fuel transfer system was placed on the internal spar of the right rear wing. Immediately above that same spar sat the radio equipment. Any spark from the transmitter could ignite spilled fuel.

Adding to this accident waiting to happen was the fact that flight crews often smoked cigarettes while on missions. Unlike today's airplanes that observe a non-smoking policy, aircraft—especially military aircraft—of that era were operated by GIs who were products of a society that accepted cigarette smoking as just a part of growing up.

Yielding to pressure from his staff, President Roosevelt used for his official trips trains, ships or commercial airliners. The White House continued to use *The Cow* (as it was now known) to transport the First Lady, Eleanor Roosevelt, who traveled throughout the world visiting military personnel on the fronts and conducting other goodwill tours during the last months of World War II.

A Comment from On High

The Sacred Cow was not equipped for combat. President Harry Truman, however, was known to use it for aggressive tactics. Once, when the entire White House staff, including his family, went outside onto the roof of the Executive Mansion to watch an air show over the nation's capital, President Truman was flying home. He ordered his pilot to "buzz" the White House at 500 feet. A startled Mrs. Truman, daughter Margaret and the rest of the staff were surprised not only to see *The Sacred Cow* fly so close, but also the President, himself, waving from a side window of the plane.

On a flight from Washington, D.C. to Kansas City, Truman ordered his pilot to inform him when the aircraft would be passing over Ohio—the state represented by his political archrival, conservative Republican Sen. Robert Taft. As soon as the captain informed Truman that they had crossed the Ohio border, the President went to the nearest lavatory aboard the plane to relieve himself. When he returned to his seat in the cabin, Mr. Truman ordered that the disposal system be activated so that its entire contents would be dumped onto the waiting ground of Ohio.

The First President to Fly

President Theodore Roosevelt was a tough hombre, as exemplified by his military career as a leader of the legendary "Rough Riders." Even the name of the political party he formed—"The Bull Moose Party"—had the ring of machoism.

In line with his spirit of adventure, Roosevelt was the first sitting President of the United States to fly in an airplane. During an air show at Aviation Field in St. Louis on October 11, 1910, he climbed aboard an airplane similar to the one built by the Wright brothers seven years earlier. The plane, piloted by Arch Hoxspy, climbed 50 feet into the air, circled the field twice and landed after four minutes.

Roosevelt was thrilled with the experience. He publicly supported the use of aircraft in war and was one of the first to promote the theory that aircraft could even fly from the decks of battleships. This came from a man whose own son, Kermit, a World War I fighter pilot, was killed in 1918.

Perhaps his best praise for aviation and for those who braved the skies was given several years following his term of office in Washington, at a banquet honoring World War I veterans: "The ordinary air fighter is an extraordinary man, and the extraordinary air fighter stands as one in a million among his fellows."

Protocol

After Western Airlines was founded in 1926—as Western Air Express—the first pilot hired was a slim, ex-army Airman named Fred W. Kelly, an exuberant Irishman known mostly for his pranks. Lieutenant Kelly had been stationed at Mitchell Field, Long Island, after World War I and learned that President Woodrow Wilson was leaving New York that very day on the liner U.S.S. *George Washington* to attend the Paris peace talks.

"I need some flight time," Kelly told his commanding officer that afternoon. "May I take the Jenny up for an hour or so?"

His unsuspecting commander granted permission, never dreaming what Kelly had in mind for a flight plan.

Kelly took off and quickly located the big liner just as it was leaving the dock, her twin stacks belching clouds of black smoke. Overcome by an irresistible urge to mess up that symmetrical smoke, Kelly buzzed the ship so closely that he not only left the smoke columns in swirling disintegration, but almost hit the radio antenna wires suspended between the two masts.

To compound this felony, Kelly proceeded to fly under every bridge on the East River. Inevitably, witnesses spotted the Jenny's wing number. When Kelly landed, he was greeted by his near-frazzled commanding officer, who demanded an explanation.

A Curtiss JN-4 "Jenny" is refueled.
Photo courtesy of Octave Chanute Aerospace Museum

Kelly's excuse deserves to go down in history along with such classic military quotes as Custer's "We've got 'em corncred, boys." Kelly merely exited the plane, stood in front of his CO, sharply saluted, and said, "Sir, I just wanted to say 'goodbye' to the President."

Our Comforter-in-Chief

When the spaceship *Challenger* that included Christa McAuliffe, the first teacher in space, exploded one minute after liftoff on January 28, 1986, a somber President Ronald Reagan spoke to the nation. From the Oval Office he looked into the eye of the television camera and captured the mindset of those who had perished just a few hours earlier. He spoke first to their families: "Your loved ones were daring and brave, and they had that special grace, that special spirit that says, 'Give me a challenge and I'll meet it with joy.' They had a hunger to explore the universe and discover its truths."

The president also remembered a special group of citizens: "I want to say something to the schoolchildren of America who were watching the live coverage of the shuttle's takeoff. I know it is hard to understand, but sometimes painful things like this happen. It's all part of the process of exploration and discovery. It's all part of taking a chance and expanding man's horizons. The future doesn't belong to the fainthearted; it belongs to the brave."

He concluded his remarks by quoting from the famous poem *High Flight*, written by John Gillespie Magee: "We shall never forget them... as they prepared for the journey and waved goodbye and 'slipped the surly bonds of earth' to 'touch the face of God.'"

A bit more than 17 years later, the voyage of the spaceship *Columbia* gained international attention; among its seven-person crew was Ilan Ramon, the first Israeli astronaut, and Dr. Kalpana Chawla, the first Indian-born woman in space. Following the breakup of the craft as it attempted to re-enter the Earth's atmosphere, President George Bush took the same opportunity to speak with America and the world on the afternoon of February 1, 2003. "These men and women assumed great risk in the service of all humanity," he said. "Because of their courage and daring and idealism, we will miss them all the more.

"Mankind is led into the darkness beyond our world by the inspiration and discovery and longing to understand. Our journey into space will go on."

Then President Bush, unafraid to let his emotions show, quoted from the prophet Isaiah: "Lift your eyes and look to the heavens. Who created all these? He who brings out the starry hosts one by one and calls each by name, because of His great power and mighty strength, not one of them is missing."

The president concluded his remarks with a word of assurance: "The same Creator who names the stars also knows the names of the seven souls we mourn today. The crew of the shuttle *Columbia* did not return safely to Earth, yet we can pray that all are safely home."

One of the titles we give to the President of the United States is that of Commander-in-Chief of the armed forces. During the times of national tragedies such as these, however, the president is called upon to be our Comforter-in-Chief.

Part 4:

Stars Among the Stars

"The scientific theory I like best [about aviation] is that the rings of Saturn are composed entirely of lost airline luggage."

—Comedian Mark Russell

Stars. Inanimate ones cover the heavens; human stars—actors, athletes and celebrities—capture our interest here on earth. Many of these household names share the thrills and rewards of flight. These are just a few of their stories.

Be Prepared

During a warm July afternoon in 2001, 13-year-old Cody Clawson was a member of a Boy Scout group on a hike through Yellowstone National Park. Young Cody, somehow, wandered off from the group and got lost. When he failed to return, his scoutmaster called for help. Unable to find him after a four-hour search, the authorities summoned help from rescue teams in Fremont County, Idaho, and Teton County, Wyoming.

After nightfall, rain began to fall in Yellowstone. The once warm summer temperature had dropped to the mid-30s. Would young Cody be found? Would he be able to survive? Cody's mother and father, along with his fellow scouts, prayed he would be found safely.

The next morning, at approximately 8:30, a frightened, cold and wet Cody Clawson sat against a rock in a canyon hoping that someone... anyone... would spot him.

Suddenly, from atop a rocky ridge of the canyon, Cody heard the unmistakable sound of a helicopter. He wanted to wave for attention, but was too weak even to stand. All he could do was sit and hope for the best.

The pilot of the Bell 407 chopper, by pure chance, happened to spot the shivering youngster. He quickly rotated the aircraft and landed on a small ridge just a few yards away from the confused young man.

When the pilot exited his helicopter, Cody thought he was dreaming. Walking toward him and calling his name was none other than Harrison Ford. The man whom Cody knew as Han Solo in *Star Wars* and Indiana Jones in *Raiders of the Lost Ark* is a part-time resident of nearby Jackson,

Harrison Ford at the controls.

Wyoming. Ford, who has both fixed-wing and helicopter ratings, often volunteers his time to help in these situations.

Ford wrapped the awe-struck, soaking wet boy in a blanket he carried in the helicopter for just such occasions, placed him into the helicopter and flew him back to civilization, his family and friends.

"Boy, you sure must have earned a merit badge for this one," Ford said to the boy as he was flying him home.

"Guess so," replied Cody, "but I already earned this badge last summer."

"*Where Have All the Old Planes Gone?*"

Popular Hollywood actor Cliff Robertson is no stranger to the American entertainment scene. Starring in 57 major films and numerous television programs and Broadway plays, he won an Academy Award for his role in the 1968 film *Charly* and was personally selected by President John F. Kennedy to portray him in the movie *PT-109.* Earlier he had won an Emmy for an appearance on the *Bob Hope Chrysler Theater.*

Robertson is also no stranger to the aviation community. He is a licensed commercial pilot with instrument, multi-engine and glider ratings. He has owned several aircraft, including a Spitfire, an ME-108, and a Beechcraft Baron.

A popular after-dinner speaker, Robertson often quotes the following poem (copyright 1997) that he wrote. It captures his nostalgic (or is it realistic?) view of aviation:

Where have all the old planes gone?
Where have all their pilots gone?
They have flown to God knows where—
They have vanished into the air.

They have vanished, so it seems
flown away with childhood dreams.

Where have all the old planes gone?
Where have all their pilots gone?
Left their memories warm and tall
left those memories with us all.

Where have all the old planes gone?
I must fly one ere I go;
I must fly one high and low.

I will fly one last flight
unafraid of dark of night.
I will fly, but not alone—
I will fly with friends from home.
I will fly until dawn
in formation—with old planes gone.

They Will Never Understand

A Hollywood reporter once asked Cliff Robertson if the biggest thrill in his life was winning an Oscar or an Emmy.

"Neither," answered Robertson. "It was going above 26,000 feet in a glider."

The reporter was taken back by this unexpected response to his question. "What?" he asked. "I don't get it."

"Then I guess you never will," said Robertson.

Never Grow Up

Former astronaut Dr. Ellen Baker loves to tell the story about a dialogue between a schoolteacher and one of her first-grade students. "Son," asked the teacher, "what do you want to be when you grow up?"

The youngster never hesitated with his answer. With his eyes wide open and a bright smile on his cherubic face, he said, "When I grow up I wanna be an airline pilot."

The teacher raised an eyebrow and slowly shook her head. "Son, I'm afraid you can't be both."

The Baseball Star Who Lost One in the Sun

When baseball legend Ralph Kiner was inducted into the Hall of Fame in Cooperstown in 1975, fans who know the game were not surprised. Kiner may never have received the recognition he was due in the major metropolitan areas of the nation, primarily because he spent his 10-year career in relatively small markets on teams that seldom had a chance for an appearance in a World Series. Nonetheless, as the record books testify, he still holds the record for leading the National League in home runs for seven straight years. He has since earned national fame as a broadcaster (for more than 40 years) for the New York Mets.

Prior to his big-league career, Kiner served in World War II as a pilot for the U.S. Navy. During his term of active duty from 1943-1945, one incident stands out in his mind as the most memorable. This is how he tells the story:

"The United States military has been famous for putting the wrong people into the wrong places. For example, in our unit, one of the greatest second basemen of all time—Charlie Gehringer—was assigned to coach soccer, not baseball. However, I must admit that the recruiters guessed correctly when they placed me into the navy's cadet program; ever since I was a kid I wanted to do only two things in life—play ball and fly. When I was sent to flight school, I was in seventh heaven. Shortly after I completed flight training and reached the rank of ensign, I was assigned to fly a Stearman PT-17. This was, indeed, a superb biplane, one that could withstand the stress of most every aerobatic configuration—snap rolls, loops, even inverted spins.

"I never flew any combat missions during my tenure with Uncle Sam's navy. I was trained to become a submarine spotter. Frankly, I don't know how good I was in this specialty; during my 30 'missions,' I never once saw a submarine.

"Much of my active duty flying time was spent taking officers airborne in order that they might earn the four hours of flying time per month—enough to earn them an extra $75 a month (a hefty sum in those days).

"Most of these officers appreciated not only the extra money, but also the opportunity to fly in the Stearman. Hence, they showed respect for the pilot and the aircraft. In these instances, I let the passenger tell me what he wanted to do. If it was straight and level only, he got it. If the officer wanted to experience some more sophisticated maneuvers, I was only too happy to oblige.

"Once in a while, however, an 'officer with an attitude' would climb into the back seat and insist on treating both the flight and me as necessary evils. The only way this ensign could retaliate was to get the aircraft to a safe altitude as quickly as possible, then enter a slow roll, followed by a snap roll and sharp pull on the stick to aim the aircraft upward until it stalled and entered into a sharp spiral. The cocky officer eventually got sick and, as you might guess, lost his lunch—something that became his duty to clean up after we landed.

"One afternoon, an extremely surly lieutenant climbed into his seat and bellowed, 'Ensign, let's get this over with; I've got a lot to do.' I knew right away that he was a candidate for at least two loops.

"'Yes, sir,' I responded. 'First we'll go over the checklist, then...'

"'Screw the checklist,' interrupted the lieutenant, 'I told you I don't have time to waste boring holes in the sky. Now, let's get this rag-covered bucket of bolts into the air.' He paused, then asked with all the seriousness of a heart attack, 'You do know how to fly this thing, don't you?'

"An astute observer may have been able to see the steam coming from my ears. In the span of just ten seconds, he let me know that his time was more valuable than mine; on top of this he insulted both me and my airplane.

"We taxied to the end of the runway for the standard run-up. I called out the checklist: 'Controls... ignition... gas... altimeter... radio... trim... instrument panel... passenger buckled up...'

"'Say again, Ensign?' asked the caustic lieutenant.

"'Be sure you have your seat belt fastened, sir,' I said.

"'Look, Ensign, you take care of your own business; I'll look after myself.'

"*Oh boy! This guy's in for the ride of his life,* I thought.

"We took off and headed directly for the practice area. After climbing to 5,000 feet, I quickly swung the stick to the left to put us into inverted flight.

"Suddenly, I heard an eerie scream from the back seat. I flipped the plane back to its normal attitude and looked behind me to see if my passenger had gained any 'instant humility.'

"He wasn't there!

"He was gone!

"He had fallen out of the plane!

"I banked the aircraft to the left and saw the officer headed toward the ground. Although he didn't have the common sense to buckle his seat belt, he was able to deploy his parachute.

A PT-13 Stearman in an unusual attitude.
Photo courtesy of Octave Chanute Aerospace Museum

"*I'm in deep trouble,* I said to myself.

"To his credit, after he landed safely, the lieutenant confessed to my senior officer that he was the one who was responsible for his quick exit from the Stearman.

"I don't know whatever became of that officer. I would have to guess, however, that for the rest of his miserable life, he never flew in another aircraft—private or commercial—without first buckling his seatbelt."

Hall of Fame Thinking

Every baseball fan in America knows the name of Bob Feller. This fire-balling ace right-hander for the Cleveland Indians was the most feared pitcher in the major leagues. His fastball was the first ever clocked at over 100 mph. In addition, he had a wicked curve that prevented even the bravest of hitters from feeling comfortable at the plate.

Feller, who pitched three no-hitters and 12 one-hitters, won 20 or more games six times, and fanned 2,581 batters from 1936 to 1956, lost nearly four years of his prime fighting for our country in World War II in the U.S. Navy.

This Hall of Famer was also a private pilot who flew his own Beechcraft Bonanza to and from speaking engagements throughout the country following his retirement from baseball. Feller, however, was a cautious pilot. He never flew his single-engine airplane at night cross-country. On more than one occasion he was en route to deliver a speech at a banquet (for which he would earn a tidy sum of money), only to encounter a storm that prevented him from completing the journey during the day. "When that happened," he said, "I would call ahead and tell the people I would be unable to make it, and have absolutely no guilt about canceling at the last minute."

Some criticized Feller for his ultraconservative practice. This never fazed him, however. To them he had a simple response: "Birds don't fly at night. Why should I?"

Better than Sex?

Sam Wyche is one of the most respected sports personalities in America. His playing and coaching career spans 27 years in the National Football League. He played for the Cincinnati Bengals, Washington Redskins, Detroit Lions, St. Louis Cardinals and Buffalo Bills before coaching as an assistant coach with Bill Walsh and the San Francisco 49ers, then became head coach for the Cincinnati Bengals and Tampa Bay Buccaneers. He also became a successful television announcer for CBS and NBC.

In addition to his prowess on the football field, Sam is also a licensed pilot. In fact, he becomes just as enthusiastic when talking about memorable takeoffs and landings as he is when recalling spectacular runs and passes.

He once convinced his friend, Marty Shottenheimer—head coach for the Cleveland Browns, who had a television appearance scheduled that afternoon in Pittsburgh—to travel to Pittsburgh in his Beechcraft Bonanza. Shottenheimer was somewhat reluctant; he had never before flown in a private airplane.

"Ahhhh, don't worry," said Wyche. "You're really going to enjoy this. Flying is better than sex."

Sam's short motivation speech worked. Shottenheimer, still a bit unsure, climbed into the Bonanza, and the two of them took off for Pittsburgh.

NFL coach Sam Wyche discovered the joys of flight.
Tim DeFrisco/Getty Images

During the interview that afternoon on Pittsburgh's KDKA-TV, Shottenheimer was asked about his flight to the Steel City.

"Well," answered Shottenheimer, "Sam Wyche told me that the experience would be better than sex. I admit the flight was a lot of fun. But, again, I don't know what Sam's sex life is like."

The host, along with the normally stoic television camera crew on the set, burst out laughing.

Shottenheimer's editorial notwithstanding, Sam Wyche obviously gained a convert that afternoon. Shortly after his initial flight that afternoon, Coach Marty began taking flying lessons and even bought his own airplane.

Not a Pretty Picture

Comedian Dave Barry has been called the "comic's comic." He has earned a well-deserved reputation for turning a tiny thought into a full-blown monologue. This writer for a variety of shows, including the 2003 Academy Awards telecast, in an article entitled "Sex and the Single Amoebae," gave this imaginative insight as to the genesis of aviation:

"As you know, birds do not have sexual organs, because they would interfere with flight. In fact, this was the big breakthrough for the Wright brothers. They were watching birds one day, trying to figure out how to get their crude machine to fly, when suddenly it dawned on Wilber. 'Orville,' he said, 'all we have to do is remove the sexual organs.'

"You should have seen their original design!"

Before He Was Charles Lindbergh

Another story from the pen of Dr. Robert Chilcoat was about his father, Capt. Jess Chilcoat, Jr., who was a flight instructor during World War II. Captain Chilcoat was instructing at Moffet Field during 1942 near San Francisco Bay. He was directing about six of his students in solo touch-and-go landings from the control tower.

Suddenly, a BT-13 flying from outside the tower's control zone entered the pattern without gaining permission from Chilcoat. Several of the students were shaken by the unexpected aircraft that had cut in front of them. Captain Chilcoat responded to the situation by calmly directing his students to extend their downwind patterns and allow the uninvited aircraft to land.

Once he was certain that everything and everyone was safe, Captain Chilcoat turned his microphone over to another instructor and raced down the tower stairs to confront the pilot who had nearly caused a horrific accident.

As the wayward pilot shut down his airplane and was prepared to exit his plane, Captain Chilcoat leaped onto the wing of the BT-13 and yanked open the sliding canopy.

The pilot—a lieutenant—seemed startled at his "reception," and stared silently at the irate instructor chewed him up one side and down the other in language not heard at the local Methodist Sunday School.

After a few minutes, Chilcoat calmed down. The pilot calmly apologized for disrupting the pattern. He had be-

*Jimmy Stewart in uniform, a tribute to Hollywood
stars who did their wartime duty. AP/WWP*

lieved that he had been cleared into the pattern. As it turned out, however, he was lost and should have been landing at another nearby field. He had been cleared to land on, of course, another frequency.

Captain Chilcoat began to get the picture. But as he listened to the pilot's explanation, he got the distinct feeling that he had seen the young lieutenant someplace before. After several minutes, it dawned on him. The lieutenant was none other than actor James Stewart, who had joined the Army Air Corps a few months earlier amid a great deal of attendant publicity. He was working through pilot training as would any other cadet.

Captain Chilcoat started to apologize to Stewart for being so harsh. Stewart, however, was very gracious and explained that it was he who was at fault and fully deserved the dressing down given him by the captain.

Jimmy Stewart went on to command a bomber squadron in England, flying 20 combat missions as command pilot. He finished the war as a colonel and eventually rose to the rank of brigadier general in the Air Force Reserve. Perhaps this is why he was able to portray with such believability the struggles of a young Charles Lindbergh in his Academy Award-winning film *The Spirit of St. Louis*.

Chilcoat maintained the greatest respect for Jimmy Stewart, not because he was a good actor and famous movie star, but because he was an excellent officer who led by example, not by being a prima donna.

Johnny Carson's Great Lockout

Johnny Carson is considered by many Americans to be one of the greatest entertainers of our generation. He has been retired from public life for over 10 years, yet his millions of fans still delight in recounting his classic sketches from *The Tonight Show,* which he hosted for 30 years beginning in 1962.

Carson was, and is, a person bent on getting the most out of life. He has pursued with vigor the world of magic, of tennis and, yes, of aviation.

Once he went flying with Art Scholl, one of the world's most famous precision aerobatics pilots. Following a rugged routine of snap rolls, inverted flight and loops, Carson reported to his audience the next night: "I wanted to throw up... I just wasn't sure which way was 'up.'"

Johnny Carson eventually took flying lessons. It was after his first solo, however, as he mentioned on one episode of *The Tonight Show*, that he suffered one of the major embarrassments of his life. Rather proud of himself after mastering three touch-and-gos, he taxied the Cessna 152 to the fixed base operation. He shut off the engine, opened the door, leaped out and slammed the door sharply behind him.

His instructor, standing just outside the FBO, pointed to the tail of the plane. The rotating beacon was still spinning. That meant only one thing—Carson had forgotten to turn off the master switch. He turned and ran back to the plane, lest some erratic electrical spark start the propeller turning again and send the plane off to the wild blue yonder. When he tried to open the door, it was stuck. For some unexplained reason, when he slammed the door upon exiting the plane, the door accidentally locked. A quick call for help brought his instructor and several other anxious people from the FBO. With the aid of a screwdriver, they pried open the door and were able to turn off the master switch.

A humble Johnny Carson got into his white Corvette and drove back to his home in Malibu.

To this day, the reclusive former television star does not talk about his flying or even reveal whether he completed the private pilot course.

Back in the Saddle Again... and Again

Those who grew up in America during World War II and the Korean Conflict certainly know the name of Gene Autry. Orvin Autry (his real name) was born in Texas in 1907. Shortly after his father—a poor tenant farmer—moved to Oklahoma, young Autry's grandfather—a Baptist minister—taught him to sing and persuaded him to join the church choir. That was the beginning of the musical career of the man who would become known as "The Singing Cowboy."

The singing led to radio appearances, then to movies. His popular songs, "Back in the Saddle, Again," "Be Honest With Me" and "You're the Only Star in My Blue Heaven," were featured in his scores of movies made at Republic Pictures from 1934-1959.

During the height of his popularity, Autry enlisted in the Army Air Corps in 1942. His first duty was in Special Services, using his talent to entertain troops, attract new recruits and sell war bonds. Autry, however, had other plans. He studied hard and became a pilot. He won assignment in the Air Ferry Command, helping to transport materials and soldiers throughout Burma, North Africa, China and India.

Autry, however, had little time to rest following those long, grueling flights during the three years he was on active duty. "Nearly every place I went, invariably I'd have to perform," he said. "Even when I was in the more remote spots in India, the GIs kept hollering for me to sing. Even when I'd attempt to sneak into a makeshift shelter of a tent, someone would find me and beg me to entertain the boys. As tired as I was, I just had to do it."

When he returned to the United States, Autry was stationed at Love Field in Fort Worth, Texas. From there he flew cargo planes to the eastern areas of the country. His squadron commander at that time was a fellow named Barry Goldwater, who later became a U.S. Senator from Arizona and the Republican candidate for President of the United States.

Gene Autry logged more than 1,800 hours of flying time during his service. When he was honorably discharged in 1945, he went home, regrouped, and, two weeks later, flew off to the Pacific war theater to entertain the troops.

Following his retirement from making western movies and starring in the 91 episodes of *The Gene Autry Show* for CBS-TV, Autry became an astute businessman, the owner of several radio and television stations and owner of the California Angels Major League Baseball Team.

When he died in October 1998, Gene Autry left behind a remarkable record of service to his country.

John Travolta's Coupe

Movie star John Travolta, two-time Oscar nominee for his roles in *Saturday Night Fever* and *Pulp Fiction*, is an aviation buff—"an airplane geek," as he describes himself. He has logged more than 5,000 hours since he began taking flying lessons at 16 and earned his private pilot's certificate in 1981.

The first airplane he ever owned was a 1947 Ercoupe— a two-place, single-engine aircraft that's distinguishable by its lack of rudder pedals or flaps. That Ercoupe, by the way, is still flying and is owned by a pilot in Arizona.

Mass-produced in the mid- to late '40s, the Ercoupe was designed by Fred Weick as the first "family airplane." Weik designed the plane to be flown by the weekend pilot who would take his wife (note: women pilots were extremely rare in those days) and child on flights of fancy. Shortly following World War II, some of them were even sold in department stores such as Wanamaker's and Montgomery Ward.

Travolta still likes to talk about the good-natured, caustic comments he received from pilot friends about the unsophisticated, slow-flying Ercoupe. He still laughs when he recalls inane questions such as: "When you are flying cross-country, do birds leave dents in the rear of the tail?" Another one of his favorites was: "Do you have to file a flight plan to get from one end of the runway to the next?" Or, "Is it true that Volkswagens pass you on the roads you follow?"

Since his Ercoupe days, Travolta has "graduated" to much larger craft. He currently has his multi-engine rating, instrument rating and commercial rating. He has even qualified to be a captain for a 747. He owns his own 707, plus several other aircraft. Recently he was appointed as "ambassador at large" for the Australian-based Qantas Airlines.

Travolta and his wife, actress Kelly Preston, have a son and a daughter. They named their son "Jett." "I wanted to name our daughter 'Qantas,' but Kelly would have no part of that," he says.

The Most Competent Man

Everyone—not just avid sports fans—knows that Ted Williams was one of the greatest players in the history of Major League Baseball. Some recall that he was the last batter ever to hit over .400 (.406 in 1941) and that he was selected as a member of Baseball's Hall of Fame during his first year of eligibility in 1966.

Not many people, however, knew that Williams was also one of the better pilots in the United States Marine Corps. In fact, "The Splendid Splinter" spent five of what would have been his prime baseball years in the military during World War II and the Korean Conflict.

Williams was a wing man for none other than John Glenn, who would become an astronaut and a United States Senator. "He was the finest wing man with whom I had ever flown," says Glenn, who became a close friend of the man who wore uniform No. 9 for the Boston Red Sox from 1939-1960.

Soon after he started flying combat missions, Williams's plane was hit by anti-aircraft fire. The landing gear wouldn't go down, and he had to crash-land the burning plane. Glenn recalls, "Obviously, that shakes anybody up, but he went back to flying again. He wasn't going to chicken out on something like that."

Besides being an expert pilot and a pretty good ballplayer, the 6'3" Williams also became a record-setting fisherman. In reality, he put the Sears and Roebuck fishing department on the map by endorsing their products.

Ted Williams in his flight garb in Korea. AP/WWP

Because of his success in so many fields, veteran baseball announcer Curt Gowdy stated: "Ted Williams is the most competent man I have ever known."

Shortly following the death of the Red Sox slugger in 2002, flags flew at half-mast at Boston's Fenway Park and at the Ted Williams Hitters Hall of Fame in Hernando, Florida. Tributes poured in from the famous and from everyday fans of the Hall of Famer. Pilots throughout the nation flew "missing man formations" in honor of the passing of this legend. Perhaps Senator Glenn said it best: "There was no one more dedicated to this country and more proud to serve his country than Ted Williams."

Aviation Purgatory

One of the most popular evangelists in American history is the Rev. Billy Graham of Charlotte, North Carolina. The fiery preacher has been the spiritual advisor to American Presidents and other leaders throughout the world.

More than a half-century ago, Graham launched his first large crusades in Los Angeles, California. Through the support of newspaper tycoon William Randolph Hearst, Graham became a national figure and, in a sense, a spokesman for American religion.

One of Graham's secrets of success, so to speak, is his insistence on the importance of maintaining a deep faith while, at the same time, keeping religion—the expression of that faith—in perspective. That included sometimes displaying his sense of humor.

When Billy Graham maintained a heavy speaking itinerary that involved flying on an airplane from Charlotte through Atlanta to his scheduled destination, Graham was a guest on the old *Tonight Show* starring Jack Paar. It was on this show that Graham confessed to his host: "I am nearly convinced that after someone dies, it matters not if that person's soul is going to heaven or to hell; it'll still have to change in Atlanta."

Graham's son—Franklin—who now spearheads the ministry begun by his father, seldom has to switch planes in Atlanta, since he is an instrument-rated private pilot and often flies his own aircraft to speaking engagements.

Loneliness

Errol Mann, former NFL kicker, has something that few pro football players share. As a member of the world champion Oakland Raiders, Errol owns a ring resulting from a Super Bowl victory over Minnesota on January 9, 1977.

Errol is proud of that ring. He's also proud of the fact that he is one of the rare pilots who built his own airplane—a Rutan Long-EZ.

After Errol had completed the construction on his airplane in 1991, he towed it out to a grass strip in Bozeman, Montana, for its initial flight.

In professional football, experts claim that there is no lonelier feeling in the world than that known to a place kicker who must kick a game-tying field goal or extra point when no time remains on the clock. Errol would disagree with that. He explains why.

"I climbed into the composite-covered airplane, fired up the engine, pushed the throttle forward and lifted off. I have to tell you one thing. The moment the plane left the ground, I experienced the loneliest feeling known to man. I was alone in an airplane I built. A successful flight and my survival depended solely upon my skills as a pilot and as a builder. I had no one else to bank on."

Outside these unique anxieties, the first solo was uneventful. Yet, even compared with the time he was flying and his engine quit, this was the most awesome experience he has ever felt.

It was almost as uplifting as winning a Super Bowl ring.

Part 5:

Our Healthy Respect for Flying

*"There are old pilots, and there are bold pilots.
But there are no old, bold pilots."*
— Attributed to W.W. Windstaff,
an American who flew with the British RFC

One of the all-time half-truths in aviation or in any other endeavor is that pilots fear nothing. Nuts! Every time an aviator lifts an aircraft off the runway, he or she enters an element that is totally unforgiving. As a result, every pilot, with every takeoff, experiences some anxiety.

But that's not necessarily a bad omen. In fact, it's a positive sign.

One of the best commentaries on this was expressed in one of my favorite movies: *The Great Santini*. In one scene, someone asks Lt. Col. Bull Meecham, "Are you ever afraid when you fly?"

"That's a good question," answered the seasoned Marine. "Yeah. I'm always a little afraid when I fly. That's what makes me so damn good. I've seen pilots who weren't afraid of anything, who would forget about checking their instruments, who flew by instinct as though they were immortal. I've pissed on the graves of those poor bastards, too. The pilot who isn't a little bit afraid always screws up, and when you screw up bad in a jet, you get a corporal playing taps at the expense of the government."

But I said that lack of fear was a half-truth, because every good pilot has the potential for becoming a psychologist's dream—a textbook case of a dual personality. While a pilot, any pilot, must anticipate that something could go wrong, he or she must have absolute confidence in his or her ability to take the aircraft from point A to point B without incident. In a sense each pilot must possess the near-egocentric attitude expressed by astronaut Gordon Cooper in another classic movie, *The Right Stuff,* when someone asked him, "Who is the best pilot you ever saw?" Cooper answered, "You're lookin' at him."

The challenge facing any pilot, of course, is to know when to allow one of the two sides to dominate the situation.

A testimony that echoes the previous observation was given by Lt. Col. Robert B. "Westy" Westbrook, USAAF, who was quoted in the *Los Angeles Examiner* on June 20, 1944. "I suppose I'm as good as the next guy," he said, "but that's about all. Only reason I'm still flying while a lot of other guys are gone is because I've had the breaks so far. I believe, though, that the breaks are going to continue my way. The minute a flyer gets the notion that his number is up, he's finished. I start out, and know I'm coming back, and that's all there is to it.

"Fear? You bet your life. But it's always on the way up. Then you get to thinking about a lot of things, but that leaves you as you reach combat. Then there's a sense of great excitement, a thrill you can't duplicate anywhere. Then there can be no fear, no thought of life or death, no dream of yesterday or tomorrow. What you have at that moment is— well, it may sound strange, but it's actually fun. The other guy has his chance, too, and you've got to get him before he gets you. Yes, I think it is the most exciting fun in the world."

******

"Now there are two ways of learning to ride a fractious horse: one is to get on him and learn by actual practice how each motion and trick may be best met; the other is to sit on a fence and watch the beast awhile and then retire to the house and at leisure figure out the best way of overcoming his jumps and kicks. The latter system is the safer, but the former, on the whole, turns out the larger proportion of good riders.

"It is very much the same thing in learning to ride a flying machine."

—Wilbur Wright

"I think there is something exhilarating in flying amongst clouds, and always get a feeling of wanting to pit my aeroplane against them, charge at them, climb over them to show them you have them beat, circle 'round them, and generally play with them, but clouds can on occasion hold their own against the aviator, and many a pilot has found himself emerging from a cloud not on a level keel.

"Cloud-flying requires practice, even if you have every modern instrument, and unless you keep calm and collected, you will get into trouble after you have been inside a really thick one for a few minutes. In the very early days of aviation, 1912 to be correct, I emerged from a cloud upside down, much to my discomfort, as I didn't know how to get right way up again. I found out somehow, or I wouldn't be writing this."

—Charles Rumney Sampson,
A Flight from Cairo to Cape Town and Back, 1931

Priorities

Captain Jack Clary, a retired TWA pilot, had logged more than 36,000 accident-free hours with the Air Force, with the airline and in civilian aviation. In October 1997, just two months following his mandatory retirement from TWA, this Purdue graduate had to draw upon all of his experience to keep both his record and his aircraft intact. He's told this story at banquets and during many hangar parties.

"Around noon, I was flying alone from Chicago to my home in Daytona Beach, Florida, in my '55 Beech Baron. I was cruising at 9,000 feet above thick clouds just past Crossville, Tennessee, over the Smoky Mountains. Suddenly, the left engine started to wind down to zero power. I made several futile attempts to restart it, but nothing worked. I feathered the engine and called Chattanooga approach for vectors to their airport.

"'Are you declaring an emergency?' asked the tower operator.

"'Uh... no,' I said. 'My left engine has failed, but everything else is working fine.'

"I had just started my turn toward the Chattanooga Airport—about 50 miles to the west—when, without warning, the right engine sputtered and quit.

"After a few seconds of stunned disbelief, I radioed the control tower: 'Remember that emergency I said I didn't want to declare? Well, I've changed my mind. Both engines are now gone!'

"I advised the tower that I had a maximum glide range of 10 to 12 miles. Beneath me, I knew, were mountain peaks that I could not see. I needed a vector toward anything available within that distance. The controller advised me that Cleveland, Tennessee (HDI) was about 10 miles ahead of me.

"I elected to keep the right engine windmilling to keep the battery charged. With the peaks of the Smoky Mountains poking through the tops of the clouds and not knowing the weather underneath, I had zero chance of survival without a radio.

"The controller called off half-mile increments to the airport. After I descended into the thick clouds that made it impossible for me to see even the plane's wingtips, he skillfully guided me around the mountains that I knew were close. He added to my anxiety when he gave me the Chattanooga weather—700 feet, two miles, winds out of the northeast at 10 to 15 knots, and rain.

"To add to my woes, my only choice was runway 21 (3,300 feet) with rain, a 12-knot tailwind, and a downhill difference in elevation of 95 feet from touchdown to the rollout end. As I neared 700 feet altitude, I picked up 20 knots of airspeed. Hopefully, this would be enough to get me to the landing area.

"I broke out of the clouds at 600 feet. Two miles dead ahead was the most beautiful strip of real estate I've ever seen. I lowered the gear and flaps. As soon as I got over the end of the runway, I set the Baron down and stood on the brakes. I thought at this point that even if I rolled off the other end of the runway, at least I could walk away unscathed. Fortunately, I stopped just 40 feet from the end. I say 'fortunately,' because at the end of the pavement was a sheer drop into a 50-foot-deep ravine.

"As I coasted off the runway onto the ramp, I saw a fire truck, a state trooper's car and an ambulance in the parking lot. The Chattanooga controller, to whom I shall be forever indebted, was on the phone with the FBO to see if I had arrived in one piece.

"The astronomical odds of an unrelated double engine failure were due to fuel tank residue blocking the engine filter to the left engine, and the right engine ingesting an induction hose and blocking the air intake, causing complete loss of power.

"When I returned home, my wife asked me if my final thoughts during the descent were of her. I told her I was sorry, but my only thoughts during those last precious moments were of making sure that all the switches were in the correct position so that if they found the wreckage, no one could say: 'If that stupid son of a bitch would have done this or that, he wouldn't have killed himself.'"

******

"I could be president of Sikorsky for six months before they found me out, but the president would only have my job for six seconds before he'd kill himself."
—Walter R. "Dick" Faull, test pilot

*Captain Jack Clary had his most demanding flying moments in his
private aircraft. Photo courtesy of Jack Clary*

As a wrap-up to this section of the book, I have found some meaty expressions that could serve as models for behavior. You may wish to copy some of these words of wisdom and paste them above your desk... or even on the panel of your aircraft:

"If you don't think you're the best pilot in the business, maybe you're in the wrong business. If you think you could never make a mistake, you are really in the wrong business."
—Randy Sohn

"The pilot who teaches himself has a fool for a student."
—Robert Livingston, *Flying the Aeronca*

"There is no reason to fly through a thunderstorm in peacetime."
—Sign over squadron ops desk at Davis-Monthan AFB, Arizona.

"A pilot who says he has never been frightened in an airplane is, I'm afraid, lying."
—Louise Thaden

"If an airplane is still in one piece, don't cheat on it. Ride the bastard down."
—Ernest K. Gann, *The Black Watch*

"There's no such thing as a natural-born pilot."
—Chuck Yeager

"*Just remember, if you crash because of weather, your funeral will be held on a sunny day.*"

—Layton A. Bennett

"*Keep thy airspeed up, lest the earth come from below and smite thee.*"

—William Kershner

"*Don't ever let an airplane take you someplace where your brain hasn't arrived at least a couple of minutes earlier.*"

—Anonymous

"*I have never seen an airplane yet that can read the type ratings on your pilot's license.*"

—Chuck Boedecker

While you are flying,
there's nothing as useless as
runway behind you,
altitude above you,
gas in the fuel truck,
or a second lieutenant flying right seat.

—Old Air Force Motto

Part 6:

Communications

"If you are in an emergency situation, follow the 'Four Cs:' Climb, Confess, Communicate and Comply."
—Mike Kelly, Flight Instructor

Michael Kelly, my former flight instructor, now a captain for United Airlines, tells the story of how late one hot summer afternoon, a photographer was called by a national magazine to take pictures of one of those great forest fires that too often take place in southern California. The magazine's editor advised him that since time was limited, he would arrange for a private aircraft to fly him over the fire.

The photographer arrived at the airport just one hour before sundown. He saw a Cessna 172 waiting outside the local fixed base operation. He hopped into the right seat of the plane and placed his equipment on the back seat.

"Let's go," he shouted to the young man in the pilot's seat. Even before the photographer had the time to buckle his seat belt, his companion started the engine and headed the plane to the runway. Within minutes, they were aloft.

"Fly over the west side of the fire," said the photographer, "and make a few low passes."

"Why should we do that?" asked the pilot.

"Well... because I want to take some good pictures," yelled the photographer in a caustic tone that showed his frustration. "I'm a photographer, and photographers are supposed to take pictures."

"Photographer?" asked a now nervous pilot. "You mean you're not a flight instructor?"

Strange but True Laws About Women and Aviation

It is against the law for a pilot to tickle a female flying student under her chin with a feather duster in order to get her attention. (Columbia, Pennsylvania)

No female shall appear in a bathing suit at any airport in this state unless she is escorted by two officers or unless she is armed with a club. The provisions of this statute shall not apply to females weighing less than 90 pounds nor exceeding 200 pounds, nor shall it apply to female horses. (Kentucky)

Women who are single, widowed, or divorced are banned from parachuting on Sunday. (Crawford, Nebraska)

No flying instructor "can place his arm around a woman without a good and lawful reason" while flying.   (Rock Springs, Wyoming)

Lingerie can't be hung on a clothesline at the airport unless the undies are carefully hidden from prying eyes by a "suitable screen." (Kidderville, New Hampshire)

*A Cessna 172, such as many student pilots learn in, sits outside
its hangar at Fulton County Airport in Rochester, In.
Photo courtesy of the Mentone Flying Club*

She Floored the Champ

Dr. George Manning, professor of psychology at Northern Kentucky University, loves to tell the story about one of the world's most recognized personalities—Muhammad Ali—who had entered the passenger cabin just prior to the closing of the doors for an Eastern Airlines flight from Atlanta to Los Angeles. As the L-1011 taxied toward the runway, one of the flight attendants approached the former heavyweight champion and, so as not to embarrass him in front of the other passengers, advised him in a whisper, "Mr. Ali, please buckle your seatbelt."

The dapperly dressed Ali looked at her with almost angelic eyes and asked, "Pardon me, I couldn't hear you. What did you say?"

The flight attendant replied in a voice loud enough for everyone to hear, "Sir, please buckle your seatbelt."

Ali flashed her his famous winsome smile and pronounced in his raspy voice, "Superman don't need no seatbelt." He grinned broadly as his fellow passengers laughed loudly.

Not to be outdone, the flight attendant drew herself up to her full 5'4" height and said, "Superman don't need no airplane."

The passengers—including Ali—laughed with delight.

America's all-time favorite champion calmly buckled his seatbelt and nodded in appreciation to the flight attendant who was able to top one of the best.

Problems and Solutions

P = The problem logged by the pilot.
S = The solution logged by the mechanic.

P: Left inside main tire almost needs replacement.
S: Almost replaced left inside main tire.

P: Test flight OK, except auto-land very rough.
S: Auto-land not installed on this aircraft.

P: No. 2 propeller seeping prop fluid.
S: No. 2 propeller seepage normal. Nos. 1, 3 and 4
   propellers lack normal seepage.

P: Something loose in cockpit.
S: Something tightened in cockpit.

P: Dead bugs on windshield.
S: Live bugs on backorder.

P: Autopilot in "altitude-hold" mode produces a 200-
   fpm descent.
S: Cannot reproduce problem on ground.

P: Evidence of leak on right main landing gear.
S: Evidence removed.

P: DME volume unbelievably loud.
S: DME volume set to more believable level.

P: Friction locks cause throttle levers to stick.
S: That's what they're there for.

P: Transponder inoperative.
S: Transponder always inoperative in OFF mode.

P: The T/C ball seemed stuck in the middle during my last turn.
S: Congratulations! You've just made your first coordinated turn.

P: Suspected crack in windscreen.
S: Suspect you're right.

P: Number 3 engine missing.
S: Engine found on right wing after brief search.

P: Aircraft handles funny.
S: Aircraft warned to straighten up, fly right, and be serious.

P: Radar hums.
S: Reprogrammed radar with words.

P: Mouse in cockpit.
S: Cat installed.

Don't Look at Me

A combination of rain and snow pelted the windows of the commercial airliners entering the landing pattern at Chicago's O'Hare Airport. Distracting the pilots even more were the flashes of lightning that created a Halloween-like setting. Only this was not the time for "trick or treat." Instead, it was the sort of situation that justifies an airline captain's salary.

Air traffic controllers worked with caution so as to maintain as safe an environment as possible. According to several sources, the tower felt that a Delta Airlines 737 was following too close to another aircraft on final approach. "Delta, you're following too closely. Execute an immediate go-around," said the ATC.

Anyone who has been in this situation knows the inconvenience this can cause—a delayed landing, extra fuel, and passenger irritation, not to mention the need to make another approach in such ugly weather. As soon as he got the directive from the tower, the Delta captain pleaded for reconsideration. The tower operator refused. "I'll get you guys down as soon as I can," he said. "We're doing the best we know how."

Back came an unidentified voice from an unidentified pilot who accidentally left his mic switch open and exclaimed, "Bullsh—!"

The tower operator and everyone on the frequency stopped talking.

"Attention all flights," demanded the furious controller, "did you say what I think I heard you say?"

The Delta captain, knowing he had opened himself to becoming the prime suspect, kept his composure and calmly responded, "Sir, Delta didn't say 'Bullsh—!'" One of the pilots in a United 757 following the Delta flight clicked his microphone and added, "United didn't say 'Bullsh—!'"

That triggered an avalanche of reports from other aircraft in the pattern:

"American didn't say 'Bullsh—!'"

"Southwest didn't say 'Bullsh—!'"

"USAir didn't say 'Bullsh—!'"

"National didn't say 'Bullsh—!'"

Finally, the tower had had enough. "OK, you guys. You made your point. Now, please shut up while we get the Delta back on track!"

It's this kind of bawdy humor that allows aviators to keep their perspective even in the most challenging of situations.

******

Tower: "Delta 351, you have traffic at 10 o'clock, six miles."

Delta: "Give us another hint. We have digital watches!"

A Delta Airlines jet in flight.   AP/WWP

The Perfect Squelch

One day, the pilot of a Cherokee 140 was told by the tower to hold short of the runway while a DC-8 landed. He did, and watched the DC-8 touch down with a pronounced *CLUNK!* He continued to wait at the edge of the runway as the DC-8 finally came to a halt, turned around, and taxied back past the Cherokee.

A quick-witted comedian among the DC-8 crew got on the radio. "What a cute little plane," said the pilot. "Did you make it all by yourself?"

Our hero, the Cherokee pilot, not about to let the insult go by, retorted, "Yes, I made it out of DC-8 parts. Another landing like that, and I'll have enough parts to make another one."

Frustration

A student became lost during a solo cross-country flight. While attempting to locate the aircraft on radar, ATC asked, "What was your last known position?"

The student responded, "When I was number one for takeoff."

Bang!

Tower: "Ah, Boeing 747, Flight 2341, for noise abatement turn right, 45 degrees."

Flight 2341: "But, Center, we're at 35,000 feet. How much noise can we make up here?"

Tower: "Sir, have you ever heard the noise a 747 makes when it hits a 727?"

Yoo-Hoo!

At the beautiful Spruce Creek Fly-In near Daytona Beach, Florida, many of the residents make it a weekly habit each Saturday to gather alongside the runway to watch their friends and neighbors return from having breakfast at a nearby airport. On one particular Saturday afternoon the weather was perfect for flying and watching. The wind blew at only five miles per hour out of the northeast. About 50 people casually watched the returning aircraft enter the downwind pattern, base leg and final to runway five.

Among those in the traffic pattern was a Tampa-based pilot of a Cessna 310 who chose this day to visit the well-publicized community. He radioed his intentions and flew the prescribed pattern.

As the residents watched the Cessna turn final, they noticed that the plane was lined up and the flaps were extended about 20 degrees. Everything looked perfect... except for one thing. The landing gear was not down.

The aircraft was about a half-mile from the end of the runway when some of the onlookers started to wave and shout. A few flapped their arms up and down in an attempt to alert the pilot of his plight. Others waved jackets to catch the attention of the pilot.

Less than a quarter of a mile from touchdown, the pilot's gear remained up.

Now everyone alongside the runway waved frantically.

A thousand feet from touchdown . . .

Five hundred feet . . .

One hundred feet . . .

Some of the people leaped high into the air in their efforts to get the pilot's attention.

No luck. The belly of the plane sounded like fingernails scratching a chalkboard as it scraped the paved runway. Sparks flew from both sides of the airplane. The propellers came to an abrupt halt. So did the Cessna-310.

The shaken but unharmed pilot opened the cabin door and quickly exited the plane. People ran toward the crippled plane; one carried a portable fire extinguisher.

Within a few minutes, a local FBO operator drove a tow truck onto the pavement and, with the help of several volunteers, cleared the runway of the damaged aircraft.

With little more than a bruised ego and a hefty repair bill in his future, the pilot relaxed in a stuffed chair in the FBO, trying to figure out why he forgot to lower his landing gear.

"Didn't you see us wave at you?" asked one of the residents.

"Yep," said the pilot.

"Well, didn't that tell you something was very wrong?"

"Not really," said the pilot. "I just thought to myself that this must be the friendliest damn airport at which I ever landed."

Words

Words can be a jungle; words can be a garden of delight.

Words can be wild weeds that ravage the soil and rob its nutrients; words can yield a harvest of beauty and comfort, of consolation and home.

Words sloppily selected and thoughtlessly spoken can be a source of grief and contention; words well pruned and carefully chosen can be a balm to the oppressed and distressed.

For the pilot, certain words hold significant meanings.

The most peaceful are: VISIBILITY UNLIMITED.
The most adventuresome are: CLEARED FOR TAKE-
OFF.
The most tragic are: THERE HAS BEEN AN ACCI-
DENT.
The coldest are: YOU ARE GROUNDED.
The most comforting are: I HAVE YOU IN SIGHT.
The cruelest are: THIS AIRPORT IS CLOSED TO
PRIVATE AIRCRAFT.
The most regretted are: I HAVEN'T TIME TO WAIT
FOR CLEAR WEATHER.
The most hopeful are: YOUR LANDINGS ARE
MUCH SMOOTHER.
The most welcomed are: YOU PASSED YOUR
FLIGHT EXAM.
The most inviting are: COME FLY WITH ME.
The most reverent are: THE SKY.

Words. To the pilot they are special. The wrong word at the wrong time is a piercing arrow; the right word at the right time is a salve.

Soul-No

Aviation writer Jim Foreman tells the story about pilot Mark Palmer, who was towing a glider near the airport at the Air Force Academy when he suddenly smelled smoke in the cockpit. Using his most authoritative voice, Palmer called the glider he was towing: "I have an emergency here, so you'd better release."

It was later determined that he had blown an oil seal behind the propeller, and the oil on the hot muffler was filling the cockpit with smoke.

As soon as he was released from the glider, Palmer called the Academy tower and reported his emergency. He was cleared to any runway.

A few seconds later, the tower called Palmer. "Black Forest tow plane, what was your point of departure?"

"Black Forest," responded a slightly irritated Palmer, who was concentrating on getting the airplane onto the ground before experiencing any fire or explosion.

"What was your destination?" continued the tower.

Now Palmer was really getting agitated. "The Pikes Peak wave area," he said curtly.

"How many souls aboard?" Apparently, the operator was already filling out a crash report before Palmer was even on the ground.

"None. I'm an atheist!" shouted Palmer.

The questioning stopped immediately.

Mark Palmer successfully landed the airplane without further incident, found the source of the problem, fixed it, and then returned to Black Forest at minimum power.

For Better or For Worse

Famed aviation writer Robert Gandt (author of *Acts of Vengeance, Bogeys and Bandits*, etc.) tells the story of a pilot of a Delta MD-80 en route to Chicago following a long, head-banging flight through turbulence. Because of strong headwinds, the trip took much longer than expected, and the fuel supply was getting low. The pilot was weary and eager to get the plane on the ground. In short, he was not willing to put up with anyone's caustic remarks—even from the lips of a female air traffic controller.

Delta: "Chicago Center, this is Delta flight 1234 at three-five zero inbound for landing."

Center: "Delta 1234, leave three-five zero for three-one zero."

Delta: "Chicago Center, leave three-five zero for three-one zero." (Pause) "Is that at pilot's discretion?"

Center (in a tone that showed her anger): "Delta, if it was at pilot's discretion, I would have told you. Leave three-five zero and do it NOW!"

Delta: "Thank you, ma'am. Leaving three-five zero for three-one zero." (This was followed by another pause.) "By the way, wasn't I once married to you?"

Ho, Ho, Ho!

Some of the legendary erratic behavior of Western Airlines' Fred Kelly was for altruistic reasons. This became most apparent to one family in particular.

During the early days of airmail flights, a special relationship existed between the pilots and the inhabitants of isolated farms and ranches scattered along the primitive airways, especially along such sparsely settled routes such as the one between Los Angeles and Salt Lake City. In a sense, these rural folks were part of the air mail system. They were known to provide food and shelter to airmen who had been forced down near their homes. A few tended the handful of emergency landing strips equipped with government-purchased beacons.

One such family was the Bonners, who operated a farm on the edge of a desert in southern Utah. Mr. Bonner, at dusk, would turn on the lights of an emergency landing strip nearby his farm; he would dutifully turn them off at dawn.

Western's pilots knew people like the Bonners by location, rather than by name, often identifying them by the number of children who came out to wave at the mail plane roaring overhead.

Unexpectedly, Mr. Bonner died in a farming accident. The pilots found out about it and began collecting a Christmas fund for the widow and her eight children. They were especially touched by the fact that Mrs. Bonner continued to maintain those lights.

The rest of the pilots asked that Fred Kelly ascertain the kids' sizes. He accomplished this by flying low over the Bonner farm and dropping a note asking Mrs. Bonner to take a picture of the children, which she was to send to Western's Los Angeles office.

She mailed the requested snapshot, from which the pilots determined the children's sizes. A few days later, Kelly flew over the Bonner farm again, only this time he did a double take. On the roof were painted six words:

MERRY XMAS WESTERN AIR EXPRESS PILOTS

Kelly returned Christmas Eve day, dropped several packages of gifts for the children, waved goodbye, and roared away. But he had dropped low enough for everyone to see what he was wearing.

He was dressed as Santa Claus.

And No Purple Pill

Then there was the captain of the former Eastern Airlines who was unwittingly victimized by a new flight attendant largely unfamiliar with aircraft technical jargon. His flight had been delayed at the gate, and the flight attendant went to the cockpit to find the reason. The captain pointed to his directional gyro.

"I'm waiting for this gyro to erect," he informed her.

She thanked him, returned to the cabin and picked up the pubic-address microphone. "Ladies and gentlemen," she announced, "we apologize for the delay, but the captain is waiting for an erection."

The Art of Delegating

One of aviation's oldest cockpit axioms is that the distance between the left seat of an aircraft captain and the right seat of the first officer is measured not in feet, but in years. In the piston era of commercial aviation, it used to take a copilot at least eight years before he could add a fourth stripe to his uniform. Copilots spent a considerable portion of that waiting period praying (mostly in vain) that some curmudgeon captain would allow him to make an occasional takeoff or, better yet, a landing.

TWA's Dutch Halloway was no curmudgeon, and his many friends among the younger pilots included a new first officer named Bob Buck—who eventually became one of the airline's legendary airmen himself. The two flew together for six months, and Halloway kept promising Buck, "Bob, I'm gonna let you make a landing today."

However, shortly before reaching the site of the promised landing, Dutch would come up with one excuse after another. "Little too much crosswind, Bob, so I'd better take it. You can land when we reach Albuquerque." Coming into Albuquerque, Bob would be primed, only to see Halloway shake his head. "It's dusk," he'd say in a tone of abject regret. "Dusk is absolutely the worst time to land. I'd better handle it."

On the last trip of their assigned schedules, Halloway had to land their DC-2 at an emergency field in Saugus, California, because fog had closed the Burbank Airport— the flight's final destination. They put the passengers on a bus and slept on the airplane. The next morning, Dutch phoned Burbank and was told that the fog had lifted.

"Tell you what, Bob," he said magnanimously. "I'll let you make the takeoff out of here."

This, Bob Buck, reasoned, was better than making a landing, because Halloway would have to raise the DC-2's notoriously stiff gear.

The two pilots strapped themselves in the seat, ran through the checklist, and started the engines. The plane rolled down the runway. Buck eased back on the yoke. The plane got no more than a foot off the ground when Captain Halloway hollered, "Okay, I've got it. Gear up!"

The Prankster

It would take the length of a Russian novel to relate all the exploits of Capt. Simon Peter Bittner, not merely an American Airlines icon, but an airline industry legend. He was a diminutive, bald-headed man of unlimited resourcefulness and immense popularity, despite his ceaseless pranks.

Bittner began his career as a stunt pilot, wing-walker and parachutist. He launched his airline career in 1927 flying the mail in Pitcairn biplanes. When he retired in 1967, he had flown virtually every type of airplane American operated without scratching so much as a wingtip. In addition to that enviable accomplishment, he also established a reputation as the most incorrigible and feared prankster in commercial aviation history.

In truth, Bittner got away with virtually everything he pulled, and not even passengers escaped his mischief.

Cold fried chicken served in a box was standard fare for both passengers and crew in the thirties. Once, Captain Si stripped every bit of meat off a chicken leg, tied a long string to the bone, opened the cockpit's side window, and unraveled the string until the bone reached the first cabin window. Then he waited patiently for the result, which was not long in forthcoming. A flight attendant raced into the cockpit and reported that a woman passenger had gone into hysterics when she saw a chicken bone banging against the window next to her.

Bittner was rather democratic in his choice of victims.

Highest on his list of priorities, however, were young, cocky copilots. On one trip he drew one exceptionally verbose braggart who claimed to know more about flying than any captain alive—including Simon Peter Bittner.

At their layover hotel that night, Capt. Bittner happened to run into an army fighter pilot he knew who was staying at the same hotel.

"You leaving tomorrow?" asked Bittner.

"Yeah, eight in the morning," said his friend. "I'm ferrying a plane back to my base."

"Same time we're leaving," said Bittner. "Say, how about doing me a little favor?"

The next morning, Capt. Bittner let the young know-it-all make the takeoff. Just as the DC-3 reached cruising altitude, Bittner's army buddy drew up to the right of the plane. Just before the fighter came into view, its pilot rolled the plane until it drew alongside the airliner in an inverted position. Captain Bittner tapped the copilot on the shoulder and nodded in the direction of the army plane.

"Don't panic," he said gently, "but we're flying upside down."

At Least it Looked Good

In 1967, Continental Airlines was awarded a five-year contract to provide air service to the group of Pacific Islands called Micronesia; the subsidiary—Air Micronesia—was more familiarly known as "Air Mike." The initial small fleet consisted of a few DC-6B piston-engine planes. One of its first captains was George Childers, whom everybody called "Granddaddy." Like all other Air Mike pilots, he was fond of the Micronesians, although he often grew very impatient with their lack of technical skills.

At one Air Mike base, a windsock had blown away, and Childers kept requesting a new one. Several weeks had passed, and still no windsock. Finally, Childers told the Micronesian agent at the field, "Either you put up a new windsock by tomorrow, or I won't land here. If I don't land here, you won't have a job. And be certain that this one is on tight enough so that it won't blow away."

Capt. Childers came through the base the next day and gratefully noticed that a new windsock had been erected. He also noticed something else—it was pointed in the opposite direction from which the wind was blowing. On closer inspection, the captain discovered that the windsock had been welded to its pole.

Did I Say That?

The cockpit radios in the old Lockheeds were as unreliable as the cabin door fastenings, and pilots often had trouble deciphering the static-plagued transmissions from the airline's stations. The ground-to-air communications at one small station were being operated by a young woman, and the captain of an incoming flight couldn't understand what she was saying.

"I can't hear you," complained the captain.

"I can hear you just fine," she informed him.

"Well, you're just not putting out," the captain said sourly.

"I am, too," she snapped indignantly. "And I've got two guys down here to prove it."

In and Out of the Doghouse

The story is true. The name of the pilot is withheld for obvious reasons.

A commercial airline pilot was dubbed by his fellow crewmembers as "Alibi Angus" because of his ingenious explanations for every mistake he made during his airline career. His worst failing was his absolute conviction that he knew every checklist by heart; the only time he used one was when a check captain monitored his performance. On those occasions, he wore a figurative halo.

One day, when no check captain was on board, his misplaced over-confidence got Angus into deep trouble. He was taking off in a piston-engine Convair 240 and, as usual, ignored the checklist, which called for setting the fuel mixture to "full rich" for takeoff.

Angus advanced the throttles, and the Convair started down the runway. Suddenly, both engines sputtered in protest. Angus realized what he had done—or what he *hadn't* done—and shouted to his copilot to push the lever to the "full rich" position. The engines of the 240 responded, and the plane clawed skyward.

After the aircraft reached cruising altitude, one of the flight attendants entered the cockpit. "What happened on takeoff, Captain?" she asked. "A lot of passengers were scared to death. They thought we had engine trouble."

Alibi Angus didn't bat an eyelash. "I'll take care of it," he said as he picked up the PA microphone.

"Ladies and gentlemen, this is your captain," said Angus in a voice that portrayed authority. "Some you may have thought we had a little engine trouble during our takeoff roll. Actually, just as we were about to get airborne, a little dog ran across the runway in front of our aircraft, and I momentarily reduced power to let the little fella get out of our way safely. Hope you enjoy the rest of your flight."

There must have been a lot of dog lovers on that airplane, because about 20 passengers wrote the airline commending the captain for his compassion. Their letters reached the office of the chief pilot, who strongly suspected there wasn't a dog within 50 miles of that runway, but he couldn't prove it and was resigned to letting Angus off the hook.

The response did not stop there. Several of the passengers also wrote letters to their local Humane Societies about the incident, and the national office of the Society informed the airline that it was going to give the captain a special award for his deed.

Angus was eager to accept the honor, until he was confronted by the only reliable witness to the incident—his copilot. Following a heart-to-heart talk with his captain, the copilot informed the Humane Society that the captain was much too modest to accept the award and wanted to avoid publicity for doing that which any dog lover would do.

Audio Typo

The DC-3 was the first U.S. airliner to be equipped with cabin PA systems, a technological triumph that some pilots regarded as an airborne menace. For some of the more "hammy" pilots, talking to the passengers on the PA was like a stage performance. For the more introverted airmen, a PA mic could be scary.

All this brings us to the true story of a certain unnamed captain of a certain unnamed airline, who was making one of his first en route announcements: "Ladies and gentlemen," he announced nervously, "for your information we are now pissing over Pattsburgh."

Point of View

Southwest Airlines is noted for its irreverent cabin PA announcements, such as the one given recently by a flight attendant:

"This is a non-smoking flight. Those of you who insist on smoking, you may step out onto the right wing and puff away to your heart's content."

The shoe was on the other foot, however, when one of its Boeing 737s made an unusually hard landing—the kind wryly described by pilots as: "Don't log the landing time; just count the bounces."

As passengers deplaned at the gate, one elderly woman stopped in front of the captain, who was politely thanking everyone for flying Southwest.

"Excuse me, Captain," she said earnestly. "May I ask you a question?"

"Certainly," he said.

"Did we just land, or were we shot down?"

Perception

A Delta Airlines DC-9 captain suffered a fatal heart attack just before landing, and his young copilot took over, completing the landing safely. A few days later, several senior captains were discussing the incident in the company cafeteria, and one growled, "What surprised me was that we had a first officer with enough brains to land a DC-9 by himself."

At a nearby table, some copilots could not help but hear that remark. One of them looked over at the four-stripers and loudly exclaimed, "What surprised me was how the first officer knew the captain was dead."

A Fish Story

Alaska Airlines is the only carrier in aviation history to report that one of its aircraft had collided with a fish—at an altitude of 300 feet.

The flight's radio message shortly after takeoff was: "A fish just hit our windshield."

At first, the tower operator monitoring the frequency thought the pilot was hallucinating. The captain later explained, however, that a fast-climbing eagle was clutching a salmon it had just plucked out of the water, saw the airplane coming toward it and, in panic, dropped the fish.

Definition of Authority

The pilot was sitting in seat and pulled out a .38 revolver. He placed it on top of the instrument panel, then asked the navigator, "Do you know what I use this for?"

The navigator replied timidly, "No. What's it for?"

The pilot responded, "I use this on navigators who get me lost."

The navigator proceeded to pull out a .45 and place it on his chart table.

"What's that for?" asked the pilot.

"To be honest, Sir," replied the navigator, "I'll know we're lost before you will."

Part 7:

Aviation Characters

"Son, either you are the bravest son of a bitch I have ever met, or the craziest."
— An unidentified commander of Gregory "Pappy" Boyington, leader of the famed Black Sheep Squadron

Keeping It in the Family

A rather rambunctious airline captain (single, we hope) was heard flirting with one of the new flight attendants of his crew who had just been introduced to him earlier that evening.

"Hey, do you think we could go out on a date this Saturday night?" he asked.

The young attendant looked somewhat startled. "Why, Sir," she said, "you're old enough to be my father."

Without missing a beat, the sage captain responded, "You may be right. What's the name of your mother?"

Rickenbacker's Law

When he was president of Eastern Airlines, Capt. Eddie Rickenbacker had a fixation on utilization of equipment. To him, the sight of an airplane sitting on the ground was the epitome of sloppy planning and gross inefficiency. This was true even in the DC-3 days when what became known as "The Jacksonville Story" became part of the Rickenbacker legend.

One of the aircraft was parked in front of the Jacksonville terminal ready to board passengers for a flight to Chicago. Some of the passengers were just heading out to the plane when they were startled to see it pull away from the gate and taxi toward the runway for takeoff.

"What's going on here?" one of them shouted at the station manager.

"See that plane coming in for a landing?" the manager said, pointing to a DC-3 on final approach.

The passenger nodded.

"Well, that's flight 21, and Captain Eddie's on board. If he saw your plane on the ground, we'd all be out of luck. Your Chicago plane will be back in 40 minutes, after he's left."

Those Strange Moving Buildings

In his definitive history of Eastern Airlines entitled *From the Captain to the Colonel,* author Robert Serling revealed that when astronaut-turned-airline executive Frank Borman was president of Eastern, two things irritated him more than anything else. Borman, a strict teetotaler, would fire any employee—including vice presidents—who were caught drinking during working hours whether on or off company premises. The other cardinal sin was carelessness. Yet there was one time when even the colonel found humor in an incident resulting from human frailty.

Vice president Mike Fenello had the dubious pleasure of informing attendees at an executive committee meeting one morning that one of their pilots had brushed the wingtip of a 727 against the side of a building the previous night. The reddest faces at the meeting belonged to Borman and the senior vice president of flight operations, Tom Buttion— the former because he was just plain angry and the latter because to Buttion, an ex-line captain himself, pilots could do no wrong.

"Last night," Fenello intoned dourly, "at thirteen-oh-three hours, aircraft 514 damaged its right wingtip when it ran into Building 21."

Before Borman could open his mouth to fill the air with a blistering tirade, Bill Bell, senior vice president of legal and a man with a delightfully dry wit, spoke up. "Tom," he asked innocently, "was the building parked in the right place?"

Frank Borman led the laughter.

Once is Enough

On January 14, 1936, four of aviation's top executives met in Chicago, Illinois, for the purpose of framing a unified effort to promote airline transportation. Following several hours of deliberation, Jack Frye of TWA, Eddie Rickenbacker of Eastern, William "Pat" Patterson of United and C. R. Smith of American announced the formation of the Air Transport Association of America (ATA); its president would be Edgar Gorrell—a diminutive, balding corporate executive whose appearance belied his tough stance on matters he deemed to be important. Once the "Little Colonel," as he was dubbed because of his military background, grabbed onto an idea, he would just not let it go.

One of Gorrell's favorite themes was air safety. That, however, was not an emphasis endorsed by the four airline executives. In their minds, the fact that they would mention air safety could raise questions in the minds of the flying public that perhaps flying wasn't all that safe.

Chief critic of both Gorrell and his emphasis on safety was the crusty Capt. Eddie Rickenbacker. As reported by Robert Serling in his book *When Airplanes Went to War*, Rickenbacker revealed his prejudice during one of the later meetings that year when the suggestion was introduced that ATA officers should fly free on the four airlines. "I don't want them riding around free on Eastern," barked Rickenbacker to American's C. R. Smith.

Smith, who never missed an opportunity to needle his competitor, responded, "Don't worry, Eddie. They'll only try Eastern once."

An Early Christmas Present

In December 1946, a group of 29 West Point cadets decided to fly home for a short Christmas leave. Unfortunately, money was scarce. Through ingenuity, the 29 pooled their money and were able to charter a plane—a C-47 operated by Coastal Cargo Airlines. Coastal Cargo, like so many of the airlines working on a shoestring budget, was not considered by many in the industry to be a "solid company."

Nevertheless, the cadets were able to gather enough funds for a flight from Teterboro Airport in New Jersey to San Francisco, via Atlanta, Dallas, Phoenix and Los Angeles. The flight would cost each man only $110 for the round trip.

With the cadets bundled up in the converted cargo plane, the pilot left late in the evening and landed in Atlanta at about two o'clock in the morning. But when the pilot attempted to refuel the airplane, the fixed base operator in Atlanta refused. He, too, had heard of Coastal Cargo's lousy credit.

The pilot, in his attempt to help get the needed gasoline, offered the man his personal Esso (Standard Oil) credit card. The man refused to accept it for the 800 gallons of gas needed to fill the plane.

"I'm sorry," said the pilot to the 29 cadets. "I'm afraid we're going to be stuck here until the morning when I can find someone with authority to help us."

While his companions moaned at the news, one energetic cadet refused to give in. He asked for and was granted permission to use the telephone in the FBO to place a few local calls. He telephoned local emergency numbers for Standard Oil and, through a lot of fast talking and earnest pleading, was able to get the home phone number of the president of Standard Oil himself.

Robert Serling, in his popular book *When the Airplanes Went to War,* recreates the dialogue that probably took place. While the exact words may be lost, the final outcome is totally true.

"I'm sorry to bother you at this time of night," said the cadet to the sleepy president who was just awakened by the ringing phone. "But I'm in charge of a load of West Point cadets flying home for Christmas. We're stuck in Atlanta because the fixed base operator here won't let the pilot charge the gas to his airline."

"What the hell do you expect me to do about it?" the president demanded in his somewhat confused state.

"Well, sir, the pilot wants to use his Esso card, but they won't honor it."

"Who did you say this is?"

The cadet gave his name, but it meant nothing to the president of Standard Oil.

"Lemme talk to that fixed base guy," he sighed.

Within minutes, the fixed base operator was filling the tanks of the C-47.

As he started to fill the second tank, the operator called over the cadet who had the gall to place a telephone call to the president of Standard Oil in the middle of the night. "Hey, what's your name, kid?"

"Ahhhh, Borman. Cadet Frank Borman," answered the young man.

"Well, all I got to say is that you sure have a lot of guts. I predict you will have a bright future."

As insightful as the operator may have been, it's safe to assume that even he could not have envisioned that the young cadet would later command the Apollo 8 moon mission and eventually become president of Eastern Airlines.

Author Robert J. Serling still loves to spin a yarn about aviation.
Photo courtesy of Robert J. Serling

Job Satisfaction

A story is told by Captain Bryan McDaniel of NetJet about Joe, a young maintenance man who worked at the Jacksonville, Florida, International Airport. One of his regularly assigned duties was to care for incoming aircraft by cleaning the waste tanks of the aircraft lavatories. It wasn't the most glamorous job in the world. Accompanying each of his missions were filth and odors normally expected with the cleansing of such containers.

In spite of his job's obvious drawbacks, the young man performed his tasks with a spirited zeal and without flaw. In fact, he seemed quite happy performing what the military might regard as latrine duty.

His co-workers could not help but notice how he tackled his job with eagerness. They marveled at his positive approach to work and to life. One of them eventually asked him, "Joe, with your positive attitude toward everything you do, why don't you leave this job, go to school, get a degree, then go into sales or management?"

Joe seemed stunned by the question. He looked his fellow worker in the eye and asked in all sincerity, "What? And get out of aviation?"

Who? Me?

Popular aviation storyteller Jim Foreman is a respected glider pilot. Sometimes, however, he is not afraid of "pushing the envelope." He recalls, for example, one time when towing a glider in a soaring contest at Hobbs, New Mexico. Because his plane had a somewhat better climb than most of the other tugs, he cut his tow pattern short so that he would be closer to the field when the glider pilot released at 2,000 feet.

A man named Hal Lattimore, a Texas district judge in real life, was the contest manager. He quickly noticed Foreman's violation of airspace rules. Lattimore barked over the radio: "Foreman, is that you towing through the start gate?"

"Can you read the numbers on the tow plane?" asked Foreman.

"No," responded Judge Lattimore.

"Then it's not me."

A Nearly Fallen Hero

During the entire 20th century, perhaps nobody in America was more honored and idolized than was Charles A. Lindbergh. His successful solo flight from Roosevelt Field in New York to Le Bourget Airport in Paris in 1927—covering 3,614 miles in 33 hours, 30 minutes—brought accolades from around the world, including the greatest-ever ticker-tape parade throughout New York City. America and the world celebrated his marriage to the beautiful Anne Morrow—the sophisticated daughter of an ambassador who, eventually, would become America's first licensed woman glider pilot. A few years later, many of the same people openly wept when their 20-month-old son was kidnapped and murdered. In spite of this tragedy, Lindbergh dedicated his life to serving humanity, devoting himself to research into artificial hearts—at least to the perfection of workable blood pumps.

It may come as a surprise for modern readers to learn that "Lucky Lindy's" final years on this earth were marked with controversy and charges of anti-Americanism.

Prior to America's involvement in World War II, when public hostilities mounted against the Nazi government in Germany, Lindbergh accepted from Nazi propaganda minister Herman Goering the Cross of the Order of the German Eagle with Star. He raised a few more eyebrows in Washington when he announced that the German Messerschmitt BF-109 was the greatest fighter in the world.

As pressures from our government increased and resentment toward Germany grew, Lindbergh campaigned to keep America out of the war. The reason, he said later, was that he truly believed that America was not in any position to offer a serious counter to the German flying machines. Even after the Japanese attacked Pearl Harbor in 1941, he publicly sided with the isolationist group known as "America First."

Rumors spread that Lindbergh was a Nazi sympathizer. Friends forsook him. President Franklin Roosevelt expressed serious concerns about him. The press turned against him. Even the United States Air Corps refused to allow him to be inducted into the armed services. As a result, he was left to serve as an advisor to Henry Ford to get the complex B-24 Liberator into production at Willow Run Airport in Detroit.

Lindbergh—America's greatest national hero of his era—had been labeled a traitor by some and unworthy of American citizenship by many others. It was, indeed, a sad chapter in the history of the United States.

Following the war, still suffering from the slings and arrows of zealous, patriotic Americans, aside from a few consulting jobs with PanAm, Lindbergh became a recluse in Hawaii. It was there that he died and was buried in 1974.

*Left to Right: Henry Ford, Mayor John Smith, Charles Lindbergh, former mayor John
Lodge, Captain Eddie Rickenbacker in 1927 in Detroit, Michigan.
Photo taken by and courtesy of Samuel Taylor*

Excuses

Western's early pilots flew the mail between Los Angeles and Salt Lake City, the airline's only route at the time, and the pilots needed an occasional shenanigan—as dictated by the gospel according to Fred W. Kelly, the loveable Irish leprechaun among their pilots—to relieve the boredom of lonely flights and as an antidote to the constant dangers they faced. Kelly and the next three pilots the airline hired quickly dubbed themselves "The Four Horsemen." Kelly was the ringleader.

This quartet, along with the brethren who joined them later, would behave themselves in the event that they were carrying some intrepid and extremely rare passenger willing to ride on top of mail sacks. But on solo trips, they would buzz herds of wild horses and shoot at coyotes with the revolvers every air mail pilot was required to carry. Chasing trains was another relished form of entertainment, particularly if there was a stiff headwind. The technique was to fly low and slow until they were abreast of the locomotive, then wave at the startled engineer and fireman.

The eastbound and westbound mail flights often passed each other. Because there were no two-way radios available to airmen in those days, pilots devised a method of sending a "Let's land" signal; it consisted of one plane waggling its wings. Usually it meant that the signaling pilot had an interesting passenger on board.

One day, the eastbound Kelly saw the signal from his

westbound colleague Jimmy James. Both planes landed on a desert strip, where James introduced Kelly to his passenger, film star Ben Lyons. The three of them chatted for more than an hour before resuming their flights—James heading home to Los Angeles and Kelly to Salt Lake City.

James was greeted by his chief pilot, a man obsessed with on-time operations. "Why are you an hour late?" he demanded.

"Headwinds," James reported.

A few minutes later, Kelly phoned the chief pilot from Salt Lake City to report that he had just landed.

"You're more than an hour late? How come?"

"Headwinds," said Kelly. "Headwinds."

Assumptions

In the first year Western operated its mail route, the "Four Horsemen" had to make 38 forced landings—25 due to bad weather and the rest because of mechanical problems. On one moonless night, Jimmy James had an engine quit on him over rugged terrain and dropped his three-minute flares, fortunately illuminating some level ground below. He landed safely, while the flares were still floating down.

A woman came out of a nearby farmhouse, screaming with rage. "You miserable coward! You left your passengers up there while you saved your own neck."

"What passengers?" asked James, rather mystified.

She pointed to the sky and the falling flares. "Why, those poor souls floating down with the lanterns in their hands."

Practice

With the introduction of wide-body jumbo jets like the Boeing 747, Lockheed 1011 and McDonnell-Douglas DC-10, flight crews had to adjust to the much higher cockpits of the huge aircraft. The neighbor of a Western captain training on the DC-10 happened by the latter's house one day and was surprised to see the pilot sitting on top of his roof.

"What the hell are you doing up there?" asked the neighbor.

"Practicing taxiing," the captain replied.

Black Tie Optional

International air travel really boomed after World War II, and this was more than a decade before jets began flying the world's airways. TWA launched its transatlantic service in Lockheed Constellations, which required the usual two pilots and a flight engineer, plus a fourth crew member—a navigator, needed because such over-water navigational devices as Loran or GPS were not yet in use.

The navigators (nicknamed "Magellans") were a somewhat clannish breed unto themselves. TWA had one with an unusual fixation—he hated to wear socks. When TWA found out about this, the navigator received a memorandum that he was required to wear socks while wearing a TWA uniform. He responded to the order by painting his feet and ankles black before each trip.

As strange as that might appear, he was not nearly as unconventional as the TWA captain who would remove his uniform upon boarding a nighttime transatlantic flight and fly across the ocean while wearing pajamas.

Part 8:

Parables

"Once upon a time, there was a king who wanted to be a pilot . . ."

In bygone days, wise men often taught by parables. These were stories never meant to be considered true. They were told not so much for accuracy of detail (although they often give us a vivid picture of those times), but to make a point.

Parables were often told to teach values, ethics, and morals. They encompass both the religious and secular markets. Parables have been told by the ancients—Jesus, Moses, David, Aesop, and Socrates; modern teachers—Mother Goose, Walt Disney, and Joel Chandler—also employ storytelling in order to teach a lesson or two.

Aviation has its share of parables. These are but a few.

The King's Lesson

Once upon a time, there was a king whose every wish was a command. To his servants he issued orders that were carried out with haste. Even members of his family responded with a sense of urgency. Wherever he went, people doffed their caps and bowed, for it was the king who had absolute power, and no one dared to disobey.

One sunny Sunday afternoon, the king announced that he wished to learn to fly an airplane. So he arranged with the most respected fixed base operator in his domain to show him what must be done.

Once inside the trainer, the king felt somewhat insecure. The controls were foreign, and the dials looked ominous. As the plane rolled down the runaway and became airborne, his anxieties increased. "Bah! Why should I worry?" he said to himself. "After all, I am the king."

At 3,000 feet, the instructor turned to his new student and said, "All right, you take the controls. Try some straight and level flight."

"Straight and level," said the king. But the airplane didn't seem to understand who was at the controls. It bobbed and weaved like an intoxicated porpoise. Suddenly, the king heard a sharp buzzing tone. The nose of the airplane pitched forward.

"Ye gods!" cried the king as he made awkward attempts to right the craft. "This machine does not respond as I command."

The plane continued to descend, until the instructor grabbed the wheel and avoided the embarrassment of an abrupt meeting of airplane with the earthly kingdom below.

"Your majesty," said the instructor, "up here, everyone is equal. Your commands, I'm afraid, are useless. You must obey the rules."

"The rules, indeed," snarled the king. "I make my own rules."

"Not up here you don't," cautioned the instructor as he brought the airplane back to altitude. "Here, you must learn them and obey them."

"Then I order you to make me a pilot," bellowed the king in his frustration.

"That's not one of the rules," answered his instructor. "I merely advise; everyone must learn, for himself, the mysteries of the sky."

At first, the king rebelled against this challenge to his authority. Yet every time he attempted to deviate from the prescribed rules, he fell from grace and the sky, only to be rescued by the quick reactions of his instructor.

Soon, however, the king suppressed his royal ego and yielded to the rules of which his instructor spoke. To his amazement, it was not demeaning; it was rewarding. He was not *subservient* to the rules as much as he was living in *harmony* with them.

For the first time in his life, he knew what it meant to be a success. Through his own efforts he shared the joys and thrills of peaceful coexistence with the sky.

Then, one day—sometime during his third lesson—without any fanfare, he removed his crown and slipped the purple mantle from his shoulders. They were necessary no longer. His instructor was right. Up here, everyone is equal.

Everyone is a king.

The Macho Pilot

(Note: The "macho" image reference is made in this story to men, although the consequences apply also to women.)

Ah, to be a "macho pilot." Wouldn't it be wonderful? Think about it. Men would follow you; women would dream about you; young children would worship you.

Exaggerated? Let's look at the facts.

As a pilot, you have a built-in "macho" appeal. People look up to you as a defier of the odds—a daredevil bent on adventure. Visions of the white-scarfed, goggled fighter pilot dance in their heads. You brave the elements and conquer them.

The "macho pilot." What a picture.

Oh, sure, the image may be blown out of proportion by someone unfamiliar with general aviation. Those of us who fly know that the one who sits in the left seat of a Cessna 172 can be a typical office worker, homemaker, sales clerk, student, or teacher. One doesn't look different from the other. Someone's personality doesn't change when earning a pilot's license.

At the same time, society (whatever that term implies) places a subtle demand upon the private pilot to "show the stuff he's made of."

For example, imagine that you and your best girl are ready to leave on a cross-country Sunday afternoon flight. Undoubtedly, she's impressed with your ability to navigate an airplane through the skies. No doubt, too, some of her admiration for you is directly related to your flying skills. But weather advisory shows severe thunderstorms en route. What do you do?

Common sense tells you to wait for the weather to clear or to postpone your excursion to another day. But no. That would be admitting a weakness, wouldn't it? So, urged on by the demands of society (that nebulous word, again) and the need to prove to your girlfriend that no "little ol' rain" is going to stop you, you forsake the warnings, push the throttle to the wall and head straight for your destination. After all, you're a pilot. You wouldn't do anything to tarnish that image.

That's macho.

The next day, your family and friends are shocked by the news of your untimely death from the accident. The NTSB report is not yet in, but everyone knows the reason for the crash. At your funeral, no one mentions this. Instead, each pays tribute to your memory.

"He was a nice guy," says one.

"Adventuresome," says another.

But it was worth it. For after you are placed into your grave, someone will inscribe on your tombstone:

"Here lies a 'macho pilot.'"

Pilot's Choice

So far, it had been an uneventful flight for the pilot en route to the small-town airport. He looked forward to a rewarding night's sleep after his long cross-country flight.

Weather advisory had predicted rain for this night, but an unexpected high-pressure system had moved in so that a strange calm engulfed the countryside.

The pilot passed over the capital city and was five miles to the northeast of his destination. It was 11:34 pm when he called ahead for landing instructions.

25T: Uh, Bethlehem Tower, this is Cessna two-five tango.

ATC: Two-five tango, this is Bethlehem Tower. Go ahead, please.

25T: Bethlehem Tower, I've just passed over Jerusalem Intersection, inbound for landing. What is your active runway, please?

ATC: Two-five tango, winds are two-niner-zero at two knots. You're cleared to runway two-seven. Report on downwind.

25T: Runway two-seven. Thank you.

ATC: Uh, Cessna, we're experiencing some interference on our radar. Please squawk 0400.

25T: Roger, 0400.

ATC: Cessna, we show some unidentified traffic about three miles to your right moving toward the city.

25T: I don't have it in sight... uh... wait a minute. I see something. It's shining. It's really bright.

ATC: Affirmative, two-five tango.

25T: Wow! Look at that. It's like a... a star!

ATC: Say again, two-five tango.

25T: A star. It looks like a star!

ATC: Affirmative, two-five tango.

25T: It's moving. No... it's still now. It's directing all of its light downward. I can see the ground very clearly. There's a barn.... And I see some men running toward it. Wow! It's weird, I tell you.

ATC: Affirmative, two-five tango.

25T: Bethlehem Tower, you won't believe this.

ATC: Say again, two-five tango.

25T: Above the light, I see... uh... some kind of beings. There must be a hundred... no, a thousand of 'em. And... they're singing. Would you believe it? They're singing!

ATC: Uh, two-five tango, are you declaring an emergency?

25T: Emerg... no. Man, you ought to see this. Wow!

ATC: Affirmative, two-five tango.

25T: The light... it's moving away. Bethlehem Tower, do you think I ought to follow it?

ATC: The choice is yours, two-five tango. That choice is yours.

Part 9:

The Feds

"If you think safety is expensive, try paying for an accident."

One of the nagging consequences of the tragedy of September 11, 2001, is that Americans have been inconvenienced in their attempts to carry on what used to be their daily routines. A striking example is the change in commercial air travel. While this used to be considered a relaxing, enjoyable experience, now this popular form of transportation is beset with an onslaught of aggravations—the chief source of which is security.

Not many years ago, the flying public only had to purchase a ticket, check luggage, then walk onto an airplane. In the early '80s, metal detectors were added in an attempt to thwart anyone with a weapon who attempted to board an aircraft. Today, because of stern directions from both the FAA and the Department of Homeland Security, passengers are met by security guards who search, search, and search again.

Many of those who currently fly the not-so-friendly skies can testify about ridiculous decisions by security guards who call aside for additional search a 90-year-old lady in a wheelchair, while allowing a 25-year-old version of Osama bin Laden to walk to the plane unchallenged.

There are other stories akin to this. Here are some of them.

Searching for What?

It was 4:30 p.m. at the Los Angeles International Airport. A member of the National Guard stood by the metal detector set up for the initial screening of passengers and their carry-on luggage. He struck an imposing figure, standing at attention in his camouflage fatigues while holding an M-16 rifle in both hands.

The guardsman smiled when he saw his replacement come through the gate; that meant his shift was completed and he could return home.

As expected, when the replacement, carrying his own rifle, stepped through the metal detector, the alarm sounded. Immediately, a civilian security agent, holding a hand wand, stepped quickly toward the guardsman and asked him to hold his arms straight out from his sides.

The guardsman did as he was instructed. One hand was empty; the other held his M-16.

The security agent moved the wand across the body, arms and legs of the patient guardsman. Once that was done, the security agent permitted the guardsman to assume his post.

I was curious. So I approached the security agent and asked, "Sir, I don't want to interfere with your work, but would you please tell me what you were looking for as you searched that guardsman?"

The agent gazed at me with one of those "You should know why" looks and, with the arrogance of a university English professor explaining to a freshman the difference between a verb and a noun, replied, "I was looking for concealed weapons."

The fact that the man he searched was holding a powerful rifle that could be seen by everyone seemed to make no difference whatsoever to the security agent.

I started to point out the lack of logic that accompanied his explanation, but, alas, I didn't think he would understand.

A Most Dangerous Weapon

Sky marshals have become increasingly familiar sights in today's commercial aircraft. While they are not detectable by the average person (after all, they're *supposed* to be working undercover) the idea that one might be on board your next flight gives added comfort to travelers in these perilous times.

At the General Mitchell International Airport in Milwaukee, Wisconsin, one sky marshal identified himself to the head of security, shared his credentials and even reminded the agent about his holster-covered revolver stored in his carry-on bag that was being sent through the X-ray machine.

An alert security agent scanned the screen in front of him. Of particular concern to him was not the .45 revolver, but something that appeared to be in the sky marshal's toiletry bag. That suspicious tiny object was a fingernail clipper. The agent asked the sky marshal to open the bag and hand him the clipper. Just as he suspected, the security agent noticed that the clipper contained a one-inch fingernail file.

"I'm sorry, sir," said the agent, "I'm afraid I can't let you board the airplane with this."

"Why not?" asked the bewildered sky marshal.

"We look upon this as a potential weapon," said the agent.

"But I've got a real weapon," whispered the sky marshal, as he pointed to the bag that held his pistol.

"Ahhhhh, well, you have a special, government-issued permit to carry that," explained the agent.

The sky marshal stood dumbfounded.

"You mean that if I want to carry my nail clipper... ?"

"Yup," interrupted the security agent, "You'll have to get another special, government-issued permit."

The sky marshal shook his head in disbelief as he zipped up his bag sans fingernail clipper.

"Any other questions?" asked the agent.

If he had any, the sky marshal didn't ask for fear he might get a response of equal intelligence.

Psssssst!

Sky marshals—those armed men and women who serve the government and airline passengers by riding on airliners—employ a standard routine to identify themselves. After letting their presence be known to the head of security in charge of screening passengers at the airport, they then report to the captains of the airplanes aboard which they're scheduled to fly. This is necessary so that in the event of an incident aboard the flight, the captain would know that the man or woman holding the revolver is a friend, not a foe.

Of course, in order that they might be effective in their jobs, the identity of the sky marshals must be kept secret from the passengers.

As part of his or her routine, the captain will then advise the head flight attendant as to which aisle seat is occupied by the sky marshal; this is necessary so that serving trays never block the sky marshal from making a quick exit in case of an emergency.

On one particular flight of an unnamed airline, the lead flight attendant forgot the row number in which the sky marshal was seated. In her eagerness to keep the row from being blocked, she called out in her authoritative voice: "Hey! Which one of you is the sky marshal?"

Any aware passenger could tell. It was the man sitting with his head in his hands, shaking it back and forth, and the look in his eyes that seemed to say: "There must be a better way to make a living."

A Conflict of Regulations

A strange case once came to the court in a small town in Southern France. The community decided to organize for its residents an arrival by none other than Santa Claus, via a helicopter. On December 24, 1989, arrangements were made with a pilot who was to drop off Santa Claus in front of the town hall. To the delight of the children and their parents, the pilot did just that. What followed was a catastrophe.

The pilot had failed to request permission from the proper authorities and was ordered to pay a fine of 1,000 francs (approximately $200). The pilot's lawyers argued, however, "How could the pilot have asked permission to bring Santa Claus if, naturally, Santa Claus's arrival is usually not announced, and no permission has ever been required by Santa Claus for centuries?"

To date, the issue has remained unsettled.

Apocryphal Letter (We Think)

Federal Aviation Agency
800 Independence Ave., SW
Washington, D.C. 20591

Dear Sirs:

I have a solution for the prevention of hijackings and, at the same time, getting our airline industry back on its feet.

Everyone knows that American air travel has been affected by the attack on our soil by Muslim extremists. Therefore, let's employ some simple logic at this point. Since men of the Muslim religion are not allowed to look at naked women, we should replace all of our female flight attendants with strippers.

Muslims would be afraid to get on the planes for fear of seeing a naked woman, and, of course, every businessman in this country would start flying again in hopes of seeing a naked woman.

We would have no more hijackings, and the airline industry would have record sales. Plus, we would provide more jobs in the workforce. In short, everybody wins.

Now, why didn't our Republican-dominated Congress think of this?

Sincerely,
Bill Clinton

Attitude

Following any incident, especially one that results in a loss of life, the National Aeronautics and Space Administration (NASA) repeats an unwritten motto that reflects the positive enthusiasm known to all pilots: "Find out what went wrong, fix it, then fly again."

Qualifications

Dear Mr. Orville Wright:

We regret to inform you that your application as a flight instructor at Zippo Aviation has been rejected by our personnel committee.

Frankly, we were stunned by your resume. The fact that your co-ownership of a bicycle shop heads the list as your longest-held job raises questions as to the seriousness with which you regard aviation. Also, we understand by your record that your first solo flight was in a homebuilt aircraft, uncertified by any government inspector. On top of this, we learned that you soloed without any prior training in a powered aircraft. Although your initial flight lasted only 12 seconds, nevertheless, this action, alone, indicates you hold little respect for proper training.

Rumor has it that your first flight was followed by several more that same day ending with an accident (caused, we think, by a combination of gusty winds and marked inexperience) resulting in severe damage to your plane. We find no record of your reporting of the incident to proper authorities.

Zippo Aviation prides itself on its excellence in aviation training. Our instructors must comply with rigid standards. In short, your background (not to mention your apparent disregard for the rules) runs contrary to every requirement of a certified flight instructor.

Indeed, Mr. Wright, we realize that you desire to fly; this has never been in question. We humbly suggest, however, that perhaps you had best consider a career other than aviation. After all, not all persons can be successful pilots.

For your own safety and that of your would-be students, we hope this personal advice will lead you to take inventory of yourself and remain in private business.

We understand that this will be a great year for bicycles.

Respectfully yours,

Zippo Aviation

Part 10:

Our Beautiful (and sometimes not so beautiful) Birds

"Just because an airplane may be made of metal, rubber and Plexiglas, we dare not conclude that it lacks a soul."
—Author Richard Bach in a lecture on"Philosophy of Flight" at Embry-Riddle Aeronautical University, 1975

More than any other means of transportation, an airplane reflects the character of the pilot at its controls. For some, such as actor John Travolta, who say: "Speed is my thing," the ideal bird is a sophisticated jet that can travel above commercial aircraft faster than the speed of sound to get to where you're going without hesitation. For others, including author/philosopher Richard Bach, a slow cross-country trip in a biplane allows them to absorb the beauty of nature and waltz among the clouds.

Pilots speak of their airplanes not as inanimate objects, but as living beings. When flying among the elements, pilot and airplane are one. It's a love affair that involves a matter of mutual trust and respect.

Some psychologists claim that a pilot never falls out of love with his or her first airplane; it's the same feeling we have throughout our lives for the first person with whom we fell in love. Of course, I shudder to think what these same psychologists would say about airplanes we rent. But that's another story. As with other loves, beauty rests in the eye of the beholder. As a result, pilots differ in their opinions as to what kind of airplane with which they want to be associated.

Here are a few stories about some of these aircraft. Many have enticed pilots into a lifelong relationship; others have left them with depleted bank accounts and broken hearts.

Pretty Good Bang for the Buck

With the millions of dollars spent today on the research for new discoveries, it may surprise us to learn how much it cost to design, construct and test-fly "The Flyer."

The United States government had given inventor Samuel Langley $50,000 to build an aircraft that could take off from a surface and return safely. On October 7, 1903, Langley attempted to do just that. Unfortunately, his aircraft crashed into the Potomac River just a few seconds after leaving the ground. Two months later, from the sand dunes of Kitty Hawk, North Carolina, the brothers Wright piloted their "Flyer" and became the world's first aviators.

When they heard how much the government spent in taxpayers' dollars, they were astonished. Including the costs of several trips from Dayton, Ohio, to Kitty Hawk, plus the amount of money spent on all of the materials, their total out-of-pocket expenses added up to approximately $850.

Humble Beginnings

How far has aviation advanced in its 100 years of existence? Perhaps this comparison will help put things in perspective.

That 12-second first flight of the Wright brothers' "Flyer" traveled 120 feet at an altitude of eight feet.

In short, man's first flight could have taken place *inside* the fuselage of a Boeing 747.

The World's Record for Underground Gliding

Before Captain Kimball J. Scribner retired in 1977 from Pan American World Airways as master pilot and chief pilot, he had the distinct "honor" of holding one of the all-time records in aviation. However, it's not one that was at the top of his resume.

Along with his accomplishments in flying a 747 and other models of aircraft, Scribner had earned recognition as the winner of the United States National Aerobatic Championship for sailplanes. All of his skill in that department was put to the test during an air show in Miami in 1951.

Kim was strapped into an open-cockpit Schweizer 1-23 sailplane and was about to be towed by an inexperienced Stearman pilot. A preliminary practice the day before eliminated any doubts as to the fact that once Scribner reached 200 feet, he would roll the sailplane 180 degrees and fly inverted. Only two bits of communication were left out of this day's flight. First, the Stearman used this day had less power than the one used in practice the day before. Second, Scribner forgot to inform his pilot that he had put water into the wings of the sailplane—something that would allow the plane to dive faster once it reached altitude.

On takeoff, the aircraft did not climb as expected. Consequently, when Scribner inverted the sailplane, he lacked the flying speed necessary to keep it afloat. The lack of speed coupled with the extra weight in the wings brought down the aircraft, with Scribner's torso hanging between the glider and the ground, in a rapid, uncontrolled descent.

Fortunately, a strong crosswind moved the sailplane to the left, and Scribner's head missed the paved runway. Instead, it hit into the much softer dirt of the apron alongside the runway. His head went into the ground and continued to move forward for 12 feet before the sailplane came to a halt.

The unconscious Scribner was rushed to a hospital. He survived the ordeal with some broken bones and a fractured neck. Through sheer willpower and the miracle of medicine, he regained full strength and health and was able to return to his position as an airline captain.

Outside of a few scars and a bruised ego, Captain Kim Scribner could always claim that he held the world's record for underground gliding.

Shoestring Budgets

In the early postwar years, America saw the proliferation of small regional airlines, officially called "local service carriers," but unofficially "feeder" airlines because their routes fed traffic from smaller cities into those of the major trunk carriers. Most of them started as shoestring operations, flying second-, third-, and fourth-hand aircraft that could have qualified for museum status.

Typical of these feeders was tiny Wisconsin Central, which, early in 1948, began serving a number of small Wisconsin and Minnesota towns with interstate flights that connected with major airline routes out of Milwaukee and Minneapolis/St. Paul. Its original fleet consisted of six ancient and sadly dilapidated Lockheed 10As, an obsolete twin-engine airplane that dated back to 1934. The airline was so short of cash that the L-10A assigned to its inaugural flight was painted only on one side—that facing the terminal building.

On one of Wisconsin Central's first trips, Capt. Bill Banks had just landed in Milwaukee and felt a discreet tap on his shoulder. He turned around to confront his only passenger, a rather shy, diffident, middle-aged man.

"Pardon me, Captain," he apologized, "but the cabin door is missing."

Banks frowned. "You mean it blew open?"

"No, sir. I mean the whole damn door fell off."

This Could Give You a Complex

A notice found at a local general aviation FBO stated: "Pilots with short pitot tube and low manifold pressure are advised to taxi up close."

Roles

A captain for TWA who stood 5'6" took more than his share of friendly razzing by his fellow pilots, so he should have been able to respond to any caustic comment about his height. However, no amount of practice could have prepared him for the comment by one of his passengers as she was entering the plane in St. Louis.

The captain, as was his usual practice, stood outside the entrance to the cockpit greeting the people as they came on board. One of the boarding passengers—a very properly attired lady in her early 60s—paused in front of the cockpit, took a hard look at the captain, allowing her eyes to examine him from his neatly polished shoes to his braided cap, then asked, "Aren't you awfully little to be an airline captain?"

Unmoved, the captain stared her squarely in the eye and responded, "Lady, I'm going to be flying this damn airplane, not carrying it."

"Often as the machine buzzed along above the sand plains, herds of wild hogs and cattle were frightened from their grazing grounds and scurried away for the jungle, where they would remain for hours looking timidly out from their hiding places. Flocks of gulls and crows, screaming and chattering, darted and circled about the machine as if resentful of this unwelcome trespasser in their own and exclusive realm.

"There was something about the scene that appealed to one's poetic instincts—the desolation, the solitude, the dreary expanse of sand and ocean, and in the center of this melancholy picture, two solitary men performing one of the world's greatest wonders."

—Bryon Newton, June, 1908, edition
Aeronautics magazine

******

"If report is to be credited, there is building on an unfrequented part of Carolina's coast an air-ship which is to put Santos Dumont's new far-famed flying machine in the blush. An Ohio inventor with two companions and fellow-workmen, it is stated, have located with their various constructive material and appliances at a quiet spot near Nags Head and have been there busied for some time in the perfection of a machine with which they expect to solve the problem of aerial navigation.

"The utmost secrecy is being maintained in regard the same and the aerial craft itself is kept within an enclosed structure. Scant courtesy is shown and but meager information doled out to the few inhabitants who have been led by curiosity to this isolated spot."

—Elizabeth City North Carolinian,
August 1, 1901

The Wright Flyer is maneuvered near its storage barn (a crude hangar).
Photo courtesy of Octave Chanute Aerospace Mueseum

Part 11:

Vision

"Our passionate preoccupation with the sky, the stars, and a God somewhere in outer space is a homing impulse. We are drawn back to where we came from."
—Eric Hoffer, *New York Times*,
on man's first landing on the moon

A famous Danish theologian, Soren Kierkegaard, was once asked by a reporter: "Are you a Christian?" To the surprise of everyone within earshot, Kierkegaard boldly said, "No!" When asked to justify his answer, Kierkegaard explained, "I am in the process of *becoming* a Christian."

In a very real sense, every pilot understands what he meant. We are never perfect pilots. We are constantly learning, growing, and appreciating.

Also, the more pilots discover the marvels of living in a three-dimensional universe, the more they become convinced that there is so much more we have yet to learn.

Therefore, every aware pilot remains in the state of "becoming."

Those who share this concept should appreciate the following stories.

Too Far Ahead of his Time?

In his book—*Fly Fast, Sin Boldly*—William Lear, Jr., writes about his father:

"My father, Bill Lear, was a visionary—always ahead of his time.

"He built the first radio that could be used in an automobile. It was this invention that set his company, Motorola, on a fast track upward to a fantastic profit. He also invented the eight-track stereo system that was the state of the art for the recording industry back in the '60s. And, oh yes, he designed and manufactured the first commercially successful private jet aircraft—the LearJet.

"Once, however, he was just *too* far ahead of his time.

"In the late spring of 1977, long after he had earned a fortune with his previous inventions, Dad became enamored with a new synthetic material that promised the same strength as aluminum at one-third less weight. It was a carbon fiber matrix impregnated with epoxy resin similar, but far superior, to fiberglass. The material was called a "composite." It had been used experimentally for various aircraft non-load-bearing structures such as panels and doors.

"Dad, never one to simply nibble at a problem, immediately foresaw a business aircraft constructed entirely from this revolutionary material. If he could design a fuel-efficient, eight-place, turboprop, all-composite aircraft weight-

A U.S. Air Force LearJet in flight.
Photo courtesy of Octave Chanute Aerospace Museum

ing one-third less than an aluminum airframe, it would have fabulous speed and climb performance, as well as increased load-carrying ability.

"In spite of the fact he did not need to take any more risks in pioneering some new concept, Bill Lear's lust for creativity blossomed again.

"The design was unique. It would be powered by two Pratt & Whitney PT-6 turboprop engines driving a single Kevlar four-bladed propeller through a specially built gearbox. Unlike conventional propeller-driven aircraft, the LearFan (as he called it) would be a pusher—a much more

William Lear discusses his dreams with his son, William Jr.
Photo courtesy of William Lear, Jr.

efficient configuration—with the engine and prop at the rear of the aircraft.

"Bill Lear died on May 14, 1978—a year and a half before his prototype ever flew.

"A lot of people, including myself, invested a heap of money—$240 million—into this project. We pre-sold 180 airplanes to people who gave firm deposits on this revolutionary product with an anticipated sales price of $850,000. I sold 60 myself, the commissions from which would net me about six million bucks.

"The LearFan concept was sound and should have been a winner. The problem was that, once again, Bill Lear sailed into uncharted waters. At this time there wasn't enough known about these new materials and the unique manufacturing process that would be required. The waters proved to be too shallow.

"The FAA was reluctant to become a party to any endorsement or approval of such a radical departure from standard aluminum construction. As a result, they kept modifying the certification structural requirements until we effectively had an airframe that weighed the same—or more than—an aluminum one. When the price of the LearFan escalated to $1,800,000, investors fled the scene, and pre-sold aircraft could not be delivered without sustaining unacceptable losses.

"Bill Lear's final dream was a nightmare. The LearFan project died. Nobody was sadder than I.

"I'm convinced that had Dad lived, he would have made the LearFan a viable program. He may have been ahead of his time, but he was no idiot, and he was not beyond compromise. Unfortunately, his followers failed to realize the significance of his great talent to convert apparent failure to success.

"At that, he was a wizard."

"The Wright Bros., two young bicycle manufacturers of Dayton, Ohio; Prof. O. Chaneut [sic], a noted scientist and aerialist of Chicago, and Dr. Spratt, a Philadelphian who has delved deep in the mysteries of aeronautics are encamped at Kitty Hawk, in lower Currituck County.

"On the bleak sand banks they have erected a machine shop and in their secluded quarters are thinking, planning, and perfecting in hopes of some day startling science and the world with a presentation, to mankind, of transportation through space."

—Elizabeth City Tar Heel
October 3, 1902

The Wright Flyer... flying.
Photo courtesy of Octave Chanute Aerospace Museum

"*Reports reach this newspaper that some vandal called a souvenir hunter has already chipped a piece of granite from the base of the beautiful Wright Memorial on Kill Devil Hill.*

"*Every one connected with this undertaking has taken something akin to a religious pride in making this monument one of the outstanding things in America. Every piece of the beautiful Mt. Airy granite used in the construction was especially selected and especially quarried.*

"*And now, unless carefully guarded it is to be ruthlessly despoiled by these loathsome creatures who must have a souvenir to tote around with them as evidence that they have visited the very birthplace of aviation. Their word for it would not suffice; people of such low mentality are such infernal liars that no one would believe them.*"

—Elizabeth City (N.C.) *Independent*,
August 19, 1932

******

"*Myth: Flight is one of the most beneficial technological advances made by man.*

"*Baloney. The airplane is and has always been primarily a military weapon, capable of horrendous destruction. The atom bomb project would never have been started if there were no airplanes to deliver them; the British and Americans in one day and night in 1945 killed 135,000 civilians in Dresden solely by use of airplanes.*

"*Illustrious men in high offices will gather Sunday at Kitty Hawk to praise Wilbur and Orville Wright and the airplane. Those who listen might well wonder why they talk so proudly.*"

—New Bern (N.C.) *Sun Journal*,
December 16, 1978

The Impossible

Over a century ago—in 1875, to be exact—the director of the American Patent Office submitted his resignation to the Secretary of the Board of Trade because, as he wrote: "We have nothing more to invent."

As a result of his fighting in fruitless battles with the Southerners, a German named Zeppelin urged industrialists to manufacture a dirigible balloon. The French Academy of Science scoffed at this as being akin to the squaring of a circle—impossible.

The idea of a heavier-than-air machine propelled by rockets was presented by Herman Gaswindt to the German war minister. After reviewing the fifth blueprint, the war minister suggested that Gaswindt be "bumped off" for promoting such an impossible dream and, thus, leading his fellow countrymen down such a hopeless path.

A firing squad eliminated a Russian named Kibaltchich who believed in and promoted the same impossible theory.

Not long ago, American scientists boldly declared that it is aerodynamically impossible for a bumblebee to fly. Unfortunately, no one ever told the bumblebee.

And so they continue *ad infinitum*—what we know as some basic elements of flight would never have been realized had everyone yielded to the opinion of the masses who deemed them to be impossible.

Several years ago, one of my students at Embry-Riddle Aeronautical University theorized that one day men and women will be able to fly even without benefit of an airplane.

Now, that's really impossible. Isn't it?

Tower Vision

It was a beautiful Sunday afternoon in early April when I flew my Ercoupe from the Spruce Creek Fly-In in Florida to the Tallahassee Regional Airport. At the same time, a constant 18 mph headwind put me a bit behind schedule. I was weary from sitting in one spot during the nearly three-hour flight and was conscious of the fact that my fuel supply was diminishing. I was happy, therefore, to see no other aircraft in the area. Six miles south of the field, I called the tower for landing instructions.

"Ercoupe, the active runway is 36. Hold your position and wait for clearance," advised the tower in a rather carefree manner. "You'll be number two to land."

Number two? I asked myself. *Why won't he give me a quick, straight-in approach now?*

I called in again. "Tallahassee Tower, I would really appreciate an immediate straight-in approach."

The tower responded with a more determined (I felt arrogant) tone: "Repeat, Ercoupe, hold your position and wait for clearance."

Now I was getting steamed. There was no reason for me to hold. I was the only one in the pattern.

I keyed the microphone in order to make known my request more strongly when my rebellious ego was suddenly catapulted back to reality. Seemingly coming out of nowhere was the largest 727 ever manufactured (at least it seemed that big to me).

Wow! Had I attempted to land when *I* wanted to, my tiny Ercoupe would have been no match bumping heads with that 727. Something like that could ruin an entire afternoon.

I guess that's why the tower operator is boss. From the position of the ATC, along with help from radar and other navigational aids, he or she can see the entire control zone.

The next time I have an important decision to make while I'm bound to the limitations of this earth, perhaps... just perhaps, instead of following just my own perspective, I would be well advised to seek the guidance of someone else who sees the entire picture.

Keep on Flying

January 28, 1986, and February 1, 2003, are two dates that will forever live in the minds and hearts of pilots. They marked the times when Space Shuttles Challenger and Columbia exploded in flight, killing all the astronauts on board.

When the death of any pilot is reported, the entire aviation community mourns. In a sense, a part of each of us dies as well. Sometimes tears stream down crimson cheeks, and confused heads shake in utter disbelief. The age-old question, "Why?" remains unanswered—hidden in some mind greater than any here on earth.

The memory of a fallen comrade weighs heavily upon our hearts; nonetheless, every pilot continues to climb into an airplane, push the throttle to the wall, then pull back on the stick to head back home to the sky.

For some, this is only therapy. For others, it helps to maintain a perspective. For a select few, it is a hope that, somewhere above those clouds, they can touch the soul of a lost friend.

On occasions such as this, aviation follows a long-held tradition that began in World War I, called "The Missing Man Formation." As a group of aircraft flies overhead, one peels off from the others, signifying the departure of a fellow pilot. At the same time, the others continue onward in a bold statement that, in spite of the recent tragedy, the mission continues.

Programmed Training

On the day after the tragic accident of *Columbia*, former astronaut Edwin "Buzz" Aldrin announced on *Meet the Press* that when he and Neil Armstrong became the first two men to walk on the moon in 1969, they were prepared to remain there, alone, without any hope of survival, had anything gone wrong.

A third astronaut, Richard Collins, circled the moon while his two comrades got their shoes covered with moon dust and gathered samples to bring back home. A reporter asked him later: "Had there been any mishap, would you have abandoned your two friends and left them on the moon?" His answer was direct: "Yes. That's how I was trained."

******

"This is all about fun. You can grab ahold of an airplane here and literally take your life in both hands. One for the throttle and one for the stick, and you can control your own destiny, free of most rules and regulations. It may not be better than sex, but it's definitely better than anything else.

"Adrenaline is a narcotic; it may be a naturally induced narcotic, but it is a narcotic. And once you get it movin' around in there, it's a rush like none other, and when this puppy gets moving . . ."

—Ann Preston, air race pilot

"Oh, that I had wings like a dove, for then would I fly away and be at rest."

—Psalm 55:6

CELEBRATE AMERICA
with These Other Great Titles from SP, L.L.C.

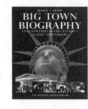

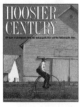